B

Be A Better READER

EIGHTH EDITION

NILA BANTON SMITH

GLOBE FEARON
Pearson Learning Group

Symbol	Key Word	Respelling	Symbol	Key Word	Respelling
a	act	(akt)	u	book	(buk)
ah	star	(stahr)		put	(put)
ai	dare	(dair)	uh	cup	(kuhp)
aw	also	(AWL soh)			
ay	flavor	(FLAY vər)	ə	a *as in*	
				along	(ə LAWNG)
e	end	(end)		e *as in*	
ee	eat	(eet)		moment	(MOH mənt)
er	learn	(lern)		i *as in*	
	sir	(ser)		modify	(MAHD ə fy)
	fur	(fer)		o *as in*	
				protect	(prə TEKT)
i	hit	(hit)		u *as in*	
eye	idea	(eye DEE ə)		circus	(SER kəs)
y	like	(lyk)			
ir	deer	(dir)	ch	chill	(chil)
	fear	(fir)	g	go	(goh)
			j	joke	(johk)
oh	open	(OH pen)		bridge	(brij)
oi	foil	(foil)	k	kite	(kyt)
	boy	(boi)		cart	(kahrt)
or	horn	(horn)	ng	bring	(bring)
ou	out	(out)	s	sum	(suhm)
	flower	(FLOU ər)		cent	(sent)
oo	hoot	(hoot)	sh	sharp	(shahrp)
	rule	(rool)	th	thin	(thin)
			th	then	(*th*en)
yoo	few	(fyoo)	z	zebra	(ZEE brə)
	use	(yooz)		pose	(pohz)
			zh	treasure	(TREZH ər)

The following people have contributed to the development of this product: *Art and Design:* Tricia Battipede, Robert Dobaczewski, Elizabeth Witmer; *Editorial:* Brian Hawkes, Eleanor Ripp, Jennifer M. Watts; *Manufacturing:* Michele Uhl; *Production:* Laura Benford-Sullivan, Jeffrey Engel; *Publishing Operations:* Jennifer Van Der Heide

Acknowledgments: The dictionary definitions in this book are from Webster's New World™ Dictionary, Basic School Edition. Copyright © 1989 by Hungry Minds, Inc. All rights reserved. Reproduced here by permission of the publisher. "The Giant Snake That Swallowed a Girl." Adapted from SOUTH AMERICAN WONDER TALES by Frances Carpenter, © 1969 by Follett Publishing Company, an imprint of Modern Curriculum Press, Simon & Schuster Elementary. Used by permission of MCP and the author's heirs. Prentice-Hall, Inc., for "Humid Subtropics." From Oliver H. Heintzelman, Richard M. Highsmith, Jr., WORLD REGIONAL GEOGRAPHY, 4th Ed., © 1973. Adapted by permission of Prentice-Hall, Inc., Englewood Cliffs, N.J.

NOTE: Every effort has been made to locate the copyright owner of material reprinted in this book. Omissions brought to our attention will be corrected in subsequent printings.

Photos: p. 29: C Squared Studios/PhotoDisc; p. 42: Bettmann Archive; p. 44: Bettmann Archive; p. 74: Scott W. Smith; p. 74: The Purcell Team/CORBIS; p. 91: Bettman/CORBIS; p. 96: Pearson Learning; p. 101: Adam Wolfitt/CORBIS; p. 102: Charles E. Rotkin/CORBIS; p. 155: Danny Lehman/CORBIS; p. 159: Bettmann/CORBIS; p. 159: Hulton-Deutsch Collection/CORBIS; p.159: Bettmann/CORBIS; p. 160: Bettmann/CORBIS; p. 160: Hulton-Deutsch Collection/CORBIS; p. 160: Bettmann/CORBIS;

Globe
Fearon

Pearson Learning Group

ISBN 0-130-23869-4

Printed in the United States of America

1 2 3 4 5 6 7 8 9 10   06 05 04 03 02

1-800-321-3106
www.pearsonlearning.com

Contents

Contents
continued

How to Use *Be A Better Reader*

For more than thirty years, *Be A Better Reader* has helped students improve their reading skills. *Be A Better Reader* teaches the comprehension and study skills that you need to read and enjoy all types of materials—from library books to the different textbooks that you will encounter in school.

To get the most from *Be A Better Reader*, you should know how the lessons are organized. As you read the following explanations, it will be helpful to look at some of the lessons.

In each of the first four lessons of a unit, you will apply an important skill to a reading selection in literature, social studies, science, or mathematics. Each of these lessons includes the following nine sections.

▶ BACKGROUND INFORMATION

This section gives you interesting information about the selection you are about to read. It will help you understand the ideas that you need in order to learn new skills.

▶ SKILL FOCUS

This section teaches you a specific skill. You should read the Skill Focus carefully, paying special attention to words that are printed in boldface type. The Skill Focus tells you about a skill that you will use when you read the selection.

▶ CONTEXT CLUES OR WORD CLUES

This section teaches you how to recognize and use different types of context and word clues. These clues will help you with the meanings of the underlined words in the selection.

▶ STRATEGY TIP

This section gives you suggestions about what to look for as you read. The suggestions will help you understand the selection.

▶ SELECTIONS

There are four kinds of selections in *Be A Better Reader*. A selection in a literature lesson is similar to a selection in a literature anthology, library book, newspaper, or magazine. A social studies selection is like a chapter in a social studies textbook or an encyclopedia. It often includes maps or tables. A science selection, like a science textbook, includes special words and sometimes diagrams. A mathematics selection will help you acquire skill in reading mathematics textbooks.

▶ COMPREHENSION QUESTIONS

Answers to the questions in this section can be found in the selection itself. You will sometimes have to reread parts of the selection to complete this activity.

▶ CRITICAL THINKING ACTIVITY

The critical thinking activity includes questions whose answers are not directly stated in the selection. For these questions, you must combine the information in the selection with what you already know in order to infer the answers.

▶ SKILL FOCUS ACTIVITY

In this activity, you will use the skill that you learned in the Skill Focus section at the beginning of the lesson to answer questions about the selection. If you have difficulty completing this activity, reread the Skill Focus section.

▶ READING-WRITING CONNECTION

In this writing activity, you will have a chance to use the information in the selection you read about, by writing about it. Here is your chance to share your ideas about the selection.

Additional Lessons

The remaining lessons in each unit give you practice with such skills as using a dictionary, an encyclopedia, and other reference materials; using phonics and syllabication in recognizing new words; locating and organizing information; and adjusting your reading rate. Other reading skills that are necessary in everyday life, such as reading a bus schedule, are also covered.

Each time you learn a new skill in *Be A Better Reader*, look for opportunities to use the skill in your other reading at school and at home. Your reading ability will improve the more you practice reading!

The Sea

LESSON 1

Skill: Setting

BACKGROUND INFORMATION

The play you will read, "Family Loyalty," tells the story of a Vietnamese family who left their homeland in 1979 to settle in the United States. After the Vietnam War ended in 1975, North and South Vietnam were reunited under Communist rule. Ongoing conflicts and poverty drove more than one and a half million Vietnamese from their homeland. Often they sailed away in tiny boats that were not made for the open sea. These refugees were called "boat people."

SKILL FOCUS: Setting

The **setting** is the time and the place in which story events occur. A story or play can be set on a city street, in a forest, or on a boat floating on a distant sea. The time can be the past, the present, or the future. Sometimes present-time events in a story are interrupted to describe an event that occurred before the story begins. This interruption is called a **flashback**. A flashback usually gives the reader some necessary background information. A writer often signals that a flashback is about to begin by having a character say, "I remember" or "I recall."

To keep track of the changes in setting for a story that contains flashbacks, ask yourself these questions as you read.

- Where does the story take place?
- When does the story take place?
- How does the time or the place of the action change during the story?
- Why is this change in setting important?

▶ Think of a story that you have read recently. Write its title in the center of the Idea Web in the next column. Then fill in the outer circles with details about the story's setting.

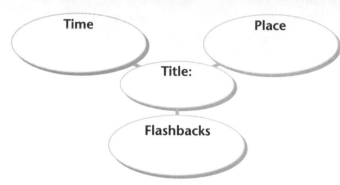

CONTEXT CLUES: Appositive Phrases

Sometimes the meaning of a new word follows the word and is set off by commas or dashes. This type of context clue is called an **appositive phrase**.

Read the sentence below. Find the appositive phrase that explains the underlined word.

The setting changes to a small boat __fleeing__, or moving quickly from, the coast of Vietnam in 1979.

If you don't know what *fleeing* means, the appositive phrase *or moving quickly from* tells you.

▶ Read the sentence below. Circle the appositive phrase that helps you figure out the meaning of *dim*.

As the setting changes, the lights on one side of the stage __dim__, or go out slowly, while the lights on the other side get brighter.

As you read "Family Loyalty," use appositive phrases to find the meanings of the underlined words *refugee*, *makeshift*, and *engrossed*.

Strategy Tip

As you read this play, watch for flashbacks that signal changes in the setting. Look for details that describe the play's two settings.

Family Loyalty

Cast

Pham Kim, known as Kim, a seventh-grade student whose family is from Vietnam

Kim's grandfather

Kim's mother

Jake, Kim's friend and classmate

Kim's father

Kim's older brother at age five

Tran Bay, a man in charge of a boat leaving Vietnam

Stranger, a Vietnamese <u>refugee</u>—a man hurrying from danger

The setting changes from a present-day suburban home in the United States to a small boat fleeing, or moving quickly from, the coast of Vietnam in 1979. When the setting is in the present, the actors are on the left side of the stage; the right side of the stage is dark. When the setting is in the past, the actors are on the right side of the stage; the left side of the stage is dark. As the setting changes, the lights on one side of the stage dim, or go out slowly, while the lights on the other side get brighter. The play begins in the present.

Scene 1

The lights slowly come up on a suburban kitchen. An elderly Vietnamese gentleman sits at the table. A middle-aged Vietnamese woman is preparing breakfast. A teenaged boy runs into the kitchen, dressed in a football uniform.

Kim: *Tieng chao buoi sang!* Good morning, Grandfather. Good morning, Mother! *(stops to look at the breakfast that his mother is cooking)* Hmmm, looks great, Mom. You know, Jake is stopping by this morning before practice. Do you have enough for him?

Mother *(chuckles softly):* The way you've been eating lately, I'm not sure I have enough for YOU!

Kim *(turns to his grandfather and speaks respectfully):* Grandfather, you remember Jake, don't you?

Grandfather *(smiles):* Nice boy, that Jake.

There is a knock at the kitchen door, and a red-headed teenaged boy sticks his head into the room. He is also dressed in a football uniform.

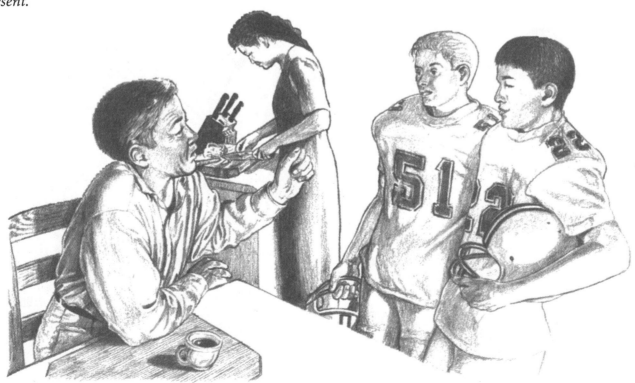

Jake: Anyone home? I could smell breakfast a block away! *(greets Kim's mother and grandfather)* Good morning, Mrs. Pham. Good morning, sir.

Kim: Jake! Great game last night, huh? Boy, you really made some fantastic plays!

Jake: Yeah, we're really coming together as a team. *(smiles at Kim's grandfather as he sits down at the table)* Mr. Pham, I've done gymnastics and cross-country running, but being on a team is special. You know, working together, everyone helping each other, putting the team first… .

Grandfather: Whether it is a family or a team, Jake, loyalty is very important. I remember when our family first began our journey to America. You were not yet born then, Kim, and your brother was only five years old… .

Lights on the left side of the stage fade out.

Scene 2

The lights come up on the right side of the stage. A small boat somewhere on the South China Sea in Vietnam is tied to the side of a <u>makeshift</u>, *or temporary, dock. It is dark, and lanterns light the scene. The boat is filled with people—men, women, and children. Kim's father, mother, brother, and grandfather are moving toward the boat. Grandfather looks noticeably tired and weakened. A man speaks to them.*

Tran Bay: *Nug lai!* Stop! The boat is almost full, can't you see? *(He points to Kim's mother and brother.)* We may possibly have room for the woman and child, but there is no room for the two men.

Father *(politely but with force, voice edged with fear)*: Please, sir, my father can no longer stay in this country! I can survive here, but he is weak and elderly. He must leave today.

Grandfather: *Thoi dii!* Enough, my son. I will stay behind with you.

Father: No, Father! You must leave now!

Tran Bay: All right. We will take the woman and child—and the grandfather. The stories of the

elderly will help preserve our past, to remind us in our new home of where we've been. *(motions to the other people in the boat)* Move over! Make room!

Kim's mother, brother, and grandfather climb into the boat. Lights on the right side of the stage fade out.

Scene 3

The lights come up on the left side of the stage. In the kitchen of Kim's home, Kim, his grandfather, and Jake are sitting around the kitchen table. Kim's mother is resting against a kitchen counter. She is *engrossed in what they are saying—giving her full attention to their words.*

Jake *(turns to Kim):* I don't understand! Your father is here with you. What happened?

Kim: Well, it was so strange! Of course, I wasn't there, but... *(turns respectfully to his grandfather)* Grandfather, you tell it.

Grandfather: In Vietnam, the family is very important. It was good for us that the people of Vietnam feel this way. I remember the words of the man who helped our family. They are words I will never forget....

Lights on the left side of the stage fade out.

Scene 4

The lights come up on the right side of the stage. Kim's mother, brother, and grandfather are sitting in the crowded boat. Kim's father is on the dock. Kim's brother is crying loudly, his arms stretched out to his father. Then a stranger in the boat speaks out.

Stranger *(stands and calls loudly):* Tran Bay! Listen to me. We cannot separate this family. No good will come of it.

Tran Bay: I want as many people as possible to leave the country on this boat, but it isn't safe to put another full-grown man on board. We're already over the limit!

Stranger: I, too, had a family. My wife and children were killed in the war. I do not know what happened to my mother and my father. All my brothers have disappeared. I know how difficult it is to live alone and isolated. *(He begins to climb out of the boat.)* Give him my space on the boat.

Father: I cannot.... *(Kim's brother again begins to cry and reach out for his father.)*

Grandfather *(looks carefully at the stranger, pauses, and then speaks):* Listen to the cries of your child, Son. Join your family in the boat.

Father *(climbs into the boat as the man steps out):* Thank you! Thank you! I cannot thank you enough!

Stranger: I will see you soon, my friend. Do not worry.

Lights on the right side of the stage fade out.

Scene 5

Lights come up on the left side of the stage. Grandfather is finishing his story. Kim's mother is placing breakfast on the table.

Jake *(sighs):* That's amazing! The man gave up his own safety so that your family could be together! I don't know many people who would do that!

Grandfather: In Vietnam, the family is everything. Here in America, we still consider family to be most important.

Mother: Yes, Jake. That is why we asked a lonely man from our country to join us when we settled here. We met him through some Vietnamese friends here in America. *(The kitchen door opens and she smiles. Kim's father walks in with another man. They are talking and laughing.)*

Kim *(gestures politely as he makes introductions):* Jake, you know my father. This is Father's business partner and my uncle, Bac Gan.

Jake *(stands to shake hands with Bac Gan):* Nice to meet you, sir. *(stares at him for a moment and then shakes his head in confusion)* Are you...?

Grandfather *(smiles):* Yes, Jake. Kim's uncle is the stranger who gave up his seat for my son. Now I am pleased to say that he is also a son of mine.

Curtain.

COMPREHENSION

1. How does Jake know Kim and his family?

   _____

   _____

2. Where did Kim's family live before coming to America?

   _____

   _____

3. What true story does Kim's grandfather tell Jake?

   _____

   _____

4. What did the stranger in the boat do to help Kim's family?

   _____

   _____

5. How did Kim's family meet the man in the boat again?

   _____

   _____

6. Circle the correct meaning of the underlined word in each sentence.

   a. The <u>refugee</u> left his homeland by boat.

   person who is very poor

   person who travels by boat

   person hurrying from danger

   b. A <u>makeshift</u> dock had been built overnight.

   temporary   permanent   unsafe

   c. She was <u>engrossed</u> in the story told by the elderly man.

   surprised and shocked

   giving her full attention to

   bored and annoyed

CRITICAL THINKING

1. Describe how Kim's life might be different if the stranger in the boat had not given up his seat to Kim's father.

   _____

   _____

2. In Scene 4, the stage directions state that Kim's grandfather looked carefully at the stranger in the boat and paused before he told his son to join the rest of the family in the boat. Why do you think grandfather paused before speaking?

   _____

   _____

3. Discuss how you think Kim's father felt about the man who gave up his seat in the boat.

   _____

   _____

4. Tell why Kim's family asked the stranger to join their family in the United States.

   _____

   _____

5. State why you think this play is called "Family Loyalty."

_____

_____

1. At what time of day does the opening scene take place? How do you know?

_____

_____

2. What other two scenes take place in the same setting as the opening scene?

_____

_____

3. The setting of Scene 2 and Scene 4 is the same. Briefly describe the time and place.

_____

_____

4. Does the action in Scenes 1, 3, and 5 take place on the left side or the right side of the stage? Explain your answer.

_____

_____

5. a. Two flashbacks in the play occur as Grandfather tells a true story. In which two scenes does Grandfather start telling different parts of this story?

_____

_____

b. Reread the dialogue in those scenes. Which sentences signal the beginning of each flashback? Circle those sentences.

Reading-Writing Connection

Suppose that you were the stranger on the boat. What would you have done when Tran Bay tried to separate Kim's family? On a separate sheet of paper, write a paragraph explaining what you would have done. Give reasons for your actions.

Skill: Reading a Timeline

BACKGROUND INFORMATION

In this selection, you will read about the sequence of events that led to the sinking of the *Titanic*. In April of 1912, the *Titanic* was the world's largest, most luxurious ocean liner. The ship's owners claimed that the *Titanic* was "unsinkable," a boast that soon proved false. On its very first voyage, the *Titanic* struck an iceberg and sank. The dramatic events surrounding this disaster have inspired many books and films.

SKILL FOCUS: Reading a Timeline

A **timeline** is a chart that shows a sequence of events in the order the events happened. Some timelines show historical events that occurred over a long period of time. Other timelines show events that occurred during a few hours or days.

Studying a timeline carefully will help you understand events in history. Each section on a timeline stands for a specific period of time. When you read a timeline, note how much time each section stands for. Then look for the dates and times of specific events.

▶ Use the timeline below to answer the questions that follow.

How much time does each section of the

timeline stand for? _____

Which ship sank two years after the *Titanic*?

_____

CONTEXT CLUES: Definitions

Sometimes the sentences around a new word contain the word's **definition**. By reading carefully, you might find the word's meaning.

Read the following sentence. What definition is given for the underlined word?

*People had thought for years that the Titanic sank because of a **gash**—a long, deep cut—in its hull.*

If you don't know the meaning of *gash,* read the rest of the sentence. It provides a definition. A gash is a long, deep cut.

▶ Circle the words in the following sentences that tell you the meaning of the word *steerage*.

*Their rooms were located in the **steerage** section—the cheapest section of the ship, that had rooms with four bunks and a washbasin.*

As you read "The *Titanic*," use definition context clues to find the meanings of the underlined words *hull*, *watertight*, and *brittle*.

Strategy Tip

As you read "The *Titanic*," pay attention to the timeline on pages 14 and 15. It will help you understand the sequence of events that took place before and after the great ship sank.

Notable Shipwrecks and Number of Lives Lost

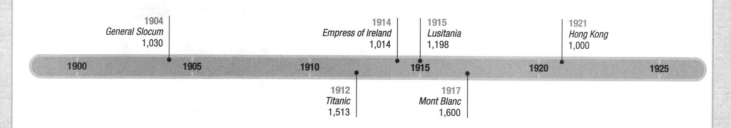

THE *TITANIC*

THE *TITANIC* MEASURED ALMOST TWO blocks long and 11 stories high. In 1912, it was the largest ship in the world. It was also considered the safest ship afloat. The *Titanic*, people said, was something new and amazing. It could not sink.

The <u>hull</u>, or frame of the ship, was divided into 16 <u>watertight</u> sections. This meant that no water could get in or out. The ship could stay afloat even if two of these sections filled with water. The *Titanic* was considered so safe that it carried only enough lifeboats for half the people aboard.

When the *Titanic* began its first voyage on April 10, there were about 2,200 men, women, and children aboard. Many of the passengers were rich and famous, like John Jacob Astor. At the age of 48, he was one of the richest men in the world. With him was his young wife, Madeleine. Also aboard were Mr. and Mrs. Isidor Straus, who owned Macy's Department Store in New York. These and other first-class passengers had rooms decorated like expensive hotel rooms. The rooms for second-class passengers were not as grand but were still very comfortable. All of these passengers could eat in fine dining rooms, exercise in the gym, and swim in the heated pool.

The *Titanic* hit an iceberg on April 14, 1912.

The *Titanic* also carried more than 700 **immigrants** (IM ə grənts), people leaving their home countries to settle in a new land. Their rooms were located in the steerage section. These rooms in the cheapest section of the ship had four bunks and a washbasin. The rooms were crowded and simple. However, these passengers, too, had much to enjoy: games, singing, even a Scotsman playing bagpipes.

Warnings at Sea

On April 14, the *Titanic* was traveling full steam ahead in the North Atlantic. The weather was clear and cool, as it usually was in April. However, the wireless **telegraph** (TEL ə graf) operator began to receive messages warning of icebergs ahead. Over the next few hours, a total of six messages came from other ships.

The captain of the *Titanic*, E. J. Smith, received some of these messages. However, he did not receive all of them. The *Titanic* had no set system for passing messages from the operator to the crew to the captain. For this reason, no one person saw all of the messages. If the six warnings had been mapped out, they would have shown a wall of ice in the path of the *Titanic*. Captain Smith simply asked the men on lookout to watch for icebergs. The lookouts could use only their eyes, because they had no binoculars with them on the lookout platform.

Disaster at Sea

Shortly before midnight, one of the men on lookout stared into the darkness. He saw a large, white shape straight ahead. The lookout rang bells and telephoned a message to the **bridge**, the platform from which the captain commanded the ship. An iceberg was directly ahead of them. The *Titanic* was headed straight for it.

The ship's officers gave orders to turn the *Titanic* so that it would miss the iceberg. However, they were too late. The *Titanic* struck the iceberg. Chunks of ice fell on the

The Titanic Disaster

1912	April 10	April 11	April 12	April 13	April 14	
	Titanic leaves Southampton, England.	*Titanic* is at sea.	*Titanic* is at sea.	*Titanic* is at sea.	**Morning** *Titanic* receives message warning of icebergs.	**Afternoon and evening** Three more warnings are received.
					Lunchtime Two more warnings are received.	**11:40 P.M.** Lookout seees iceberg and sends alarm.

plate from ship

ship's whistle

This timeline shows when events took place during the *Titanic* disaster.

deck, and the ship slowly came to a stop. In one of the boiler rooms, where the engines were located, alarms went off. A wall gave way, and water began to rush in. Captain Smith soon learned what had happened to the ship. The *Titanic* was filling up fast with water.

At 12:25 A.M., the crew rushed to call other ships for help. Ships hearing the call began to change course to come to the aid of the *Titanic*. One ship, the *Californian*, was nearby. However, the radio operator did not get the message. He had gone off duty at 11:30 P.M., the time that he usually left for the night. Then he had gone to bed.

By 12:30 A.M., as water gushed into the *Titanic*, lifeboats were lowered. Women and children were asked to get into them, but they did not know how serious the danger was. Some saw no reason to take a ride in the icy sea. Some men laughed as they helped their wives into boats. All would be well by breakfast, they thought.

The crew sent rockets into the sky, trying to attract the attention of other ships. Then the passengers began to realize that the *Titanic* was sinking. Through the sounds of shouting and crying, the ship's band could be heard playing ragtime songs. The band kept playing as the front deck of the ship was covered with water. Soon the sound of hymns was heard in the darkness.

The *Titanic* stood on end before sliding to its grave in the dark sea. At 2:20 A.M., the great, "unsinkable" ship sank in the cold waters of the North Atlantic. More than 1,500 people, including the captain, died in the disaster.

The Survivors

Some people were in the freezing water, struggling to reach the lifeboats. Most boats still had room in them, but very little effort was made to pick up the swimmers.

By 2:40 A.M., a ship had spotted the boats. By 4:10 A.M., the *Carpathia* had begun to take people aboard. There were about 700 survivors, including women, children, and some men. At sunrise, they saw the huge iceberg that the *Titanic* had hit.

Other ships racing to the rescue learned that they were too late. The *Californian,* the one ship that had been nearby, saw the rockets that the *Titanic* sent up. Yet the crew was uncertain about what the rockets meant. At about 5:40 A.M., one crew member woke up the radio operator. The operator turned on his radio and contacted another ship. He learned that the *Titanic* had hit an iceberg and had sunk.

News of survivors was slow in reaching relatives. Newspaper stories were based on only a few facts, and many reports were false. On April 18, more than 30,000 eager people waited in New York as the *Carpathia* arrived. As the survivors left the ship, they began to tell the story of the *Titanic.*

The Investigations

In the weeks following the tragedy, the United States Senate and the Board of Trade in England held **investigations** (in VES tə GAY shənz). They interviewed survivors and searched through records to find all the facts of what had happened to the *Titanic.* The reports stated that the *Titanic* had not

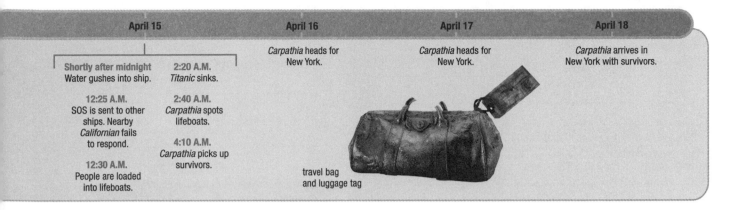

April 15	April 16	April 17	April 18

Shortly after midnight
Water gushes into ship.

12:25 A.M.
SOS is sent to other ships. Nearby *Californian* fails to respond.

12:30 A.M.
People are loaded into lifeboats.

2:20 A.M.
Titanic sinks.

2:40 A.M.
Carpathia spots lifeboats.

4:10 A.M.
Carpathia picks up survivors.

Carpathia heads for New York.

Carpathia heads for New York.

Carpathia arrives in New York with survivors.

travel bag and luggage tag

been carrying enough lifeboats. The boats that had been available were not fully loaded. Because no lifeboat drills had been held, officers were slow in loading people into the boats. If the boats had been full, at least 400 more lives could have been saved.

Investigators also found that the *Titanic* had been traveling too fast. As warnings about ice had reached the ship, the *Titanic* should have been moving at a slower speed. There also should have been more people on lookout to spot the icebergs.

Much of the blame for the lost lives went to the *Californian*. The crew of the *Californian* had seen the rockets that the *Titanic* sent up. If the *Californian* had helped the *Titanic* right away, many, if not all of the passengers, might have been saved.

Of the 2,224 people on board the *Titanic*, 1,513 drowned.

The *Californian* did not receive the calls for help because the ship's radio operator was not on duty. In 1912, the law did not require ships to have a radio operator on duty at all times.

Exploring the Wreckage

The story of the *Titanic* has continued to unfold. In 1985, a group of scientists found the wreckage of the ship. This team was led by Robert E. Ballard of the United States and Jean-Louis Michel of France. The scientists removed samples of the ship and then studied them. People had thought for years that the *Titanic* sank because of a gash—a long, deep cut—in its hull. However, the steel used in the hull was the real problem. It was too <u>brittle</u> for the cold waters. That meant that it broke easily when the ship hit the iceberg.

The explorers were also able to bring up many artifacts from the wreckage of the *Titanic*. Some of these appeared on TV shows and in a special museum exhibit that has traveled across the nation.

Many stories, articles, and films have described the greatest sea tragedy in history. In one nonfiction film made about the disaster, the wreckage of the ship is shown, more than two miles down on the ocean floor. Two submarines were used in the filming. One submarine filmed the other as it entered the site of the wreck. People viewing the film can see the remains of the ship's railing, where people stood as they waited for the *Titanic* to sink.

1. In what year did the *Titanic* begin its voyage?

   _____

   _____

2. Why did people think that the *Titanic* was unsinkable?

   _____

   _____

3. What was the reason that Captain Smith did not receive all of the messages that warned about icebergs ahead?

   _____

   _____

4. Why did the lookout ring bells and telephone a message to the captain shortly before midnight?

   _____

   _____

5. What happened in the boiler room after the ship hit the iceberg?

   _____

   _____

6. Why didn't the radio operator on the nearby *Californian* receive the *Titanic*'s call for help?

   _____

   _____

7. Trace the order of events that enabled some of the passengers to arrive safely in New York.

   _____

   _____

   _____

8. Explain why investigators blamed the *Californian* for the deaths of the *Titanic*'s passengers.

   _____

   _____

   _____

9. Discuss what scientists learned about the sinking of the *Titanic* after finding the wreckage of the ship in 1985.

   _____

   _____

   _____

10. Decide if each statement is true or false. Write *true* or *false* on the line provided.

    _____ a. A <u>hull</u> of a ship is the part that holds the sails.

    _____ b. If a container is <u>watertight</u>, no water can get inside.

    _____ c. If a seashell is <u>brittle</u>, it may easily break.

1. Was Captain Smith concerned about the safety of his ship when he received the warnings about icebergs? Explain.

   _____

   _____

2. Discuss what you think the captain expected to happen if the men on lookout spotted any icebergs.

   _____

   _____

3. Explain why the people in the lifeboats made little effort to pick up swimmers.

_____

_____

_____

4. Discuss why you think the *Californian* did not respond to the rockets the *Titanic* sent up.

_____

_____

5. State reasons why there were so many false newspaper reports about the disaster.

_____

_____

_____

6. Explain why you think the story of the *Titanic* has been retold so many times.

_____

_____

_____

SKILL FOCUS: READING A TIMELINE

The timeline on pages 14 and 15 shows when events took place during the *Titanic* disaster. Use the timeline to answer the questions below.

1. How long was the only voyage of the *Titanic*?

_____

2. For how many days were iceberg warnings received?

_____

3. When did the *Titanic* hit the iceberg?

_____

4. When were there signs that the ship had been badly damaged?

_____

5. About how long did it take the *Titanic* to sink after hitting the iceberg?

_____

6. How long did the survivors spend in lifeboats?

_____

7. What ship rescued the survivors?

_____

8. Where did the ship take the survivors?

_____

 ## Reading-Writing Connection

Read a newspaper article about an important recent event. Make a timeline to show the major incidents of the event and when they occurred.

Skill: Classifying

BACKGROUND INFORMATION

The following article, "Three Groups of Water Animals," discusses spiny-skinned animals, hollow animals, and sponges. The Earth's water is home to thousands of different kinds of animals. To understand them better, scientists have divided the water animals into different groups. Each group has important features in common that set them apart from other animals. By studying animals in groups, scientists organize large amounts of information in a way that makes sense.

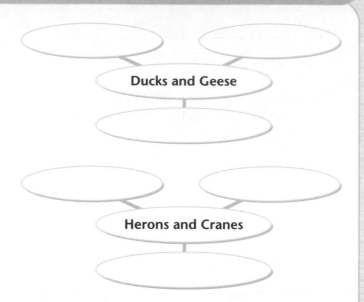

Ducks and Geese

Herons and Cranes

SKILL FOCUS: Classifying

Classifying is a way to organize information by grouping similar things together. Although you may not realize it, you classify things every day. If you were describing someone's car, for example, you might start by classifying it as an SUV, a van, a sedan, or a sports car.

When scientists classify plants and animals, they divide large groups into smaller ones. The members of each smaller group are similar in some way. Ducks and geese, for example, are similar in many ways. Both water birds are classified in the same family group. Herons and cranes are water birds, too. However, they are not in the same family as ducks and geese. Scientists put herons and cranes in a different family group.

When reading about different groups of animals, ask yourself the following questions.

- How are the animals that scientists group together similar?

- How are the animals in one group different from the animals in another group?

▶ On the first Idea Web, write what you already know about ways in which ducks are similar to geese.

On the second Idea Web, write what you already know about ways herons and cranes differ from ducks and geese.

CONTEXT CLUES: Comparisons

The words *like* and *as* sometimes introduce a **comparison** that can help you understand the meaning of a new word. Notice the comparison that helps you understand the meaning of *extend* in the following sentence.

*The starfish's body has a central disk from which five arms **extend** like those of an octopus.*

If you don't know the meaning of *extend*, the phrase *like those of an octopus* can help you. The arms of a starfish stretch out like the arms of an octopus.

▶ Read the following sentence. Circle the comparison that helps you figure out the meaning of *spines*.

*The **spines**, like the sharp needles of a cactus, protect the sea urchin from its enemies.*

In the next selection, use comparison context clues to help you understand the meanings of the underlined words *suction*, *expanding*, and *contracting*.

Strategy Tip

As you read the selection, look for the three headings. Each tells you the name of one group of water animals. Notice the similarities among the animals in each group and the differences among the three groups.

Three Groups of Water Animals

Group 1: Echinodermata

Starfish, brittle stars, sea urchins, and sea cucumbers are all members of a group called **Echinodermata** (i ky nə der MAH tə). The word *Echinodermata* means "spiny-skinned." All of these animals have a hard, spiny skin. They also have a central body from which arms, or spines, branch out.

Starfish The starfish is not a fish. A better name for it would be *sea star*. Its body has a central disk from which five arms extend like those of an octopus. Most starfish have five arms, but some kinds have a greater number. The starfish has no head. The mouth of a starfish is in the center of the underside of the disk.

The starfish has many tiny tubes on the underside of its arms. These tubes are connected to canals inside the arms. The starfish draws water into the canals through the tubes. By forcing water in and out of the canals, it opens and closes the tubes. This creates a <u>suction</u> like that caused by a vacuum cleaner. As a result, the tubes stick to a surface and are used as tiny feet. This is how the starfish moves across the ocean floor.

The starfish feeds on clams, which are slow-moving, and oysters, which do not move at all. After climbing on top of a clam, the starfish attaches its tube feet to the clam's shell, using suction. It pulls on the shell of the clam, using its many tube feet in groups, one after the other. When the muscles that hold the clam's shell together are tired out, the shell opens. The starfish then turns the lower part of its stomach inside out and extends it through its mouth. The stomach surrounds the soft part of the clam and digests it.

Certain animals are able to **regenerate** (ri JEN ə rayt). The starfish is one of these animals. This means that it can replace lost parts of its body. In fact, if a starfish is cut into several pieces, each piece can grow into a new starfish.

Brittle Stars The brittle star gets its name from the fact that its arms break off easily. However, like the starfish, it can regenerate. The brittle star crawls over the ocean floor with quick movements of its arms. Most brittle stars have five arms, but some have as many as eight. The brittle star has a mouth in the center of its underside, similar to that of the starfish. It feeds on plankton, and occasionally worms and mollusks.

Sea Urchins The sea urchin does not look like a starfish, yet it has a similar body structure. The sea urchin looks like a large ball with long, sharp spines. It moves by using its spines and its tube feet. The spines, like those of a cactus, protect the sea urchin from its enemies. The mouth of the sea urchin, like that of the starfish, is on its underside. Around its mouth is a set of five teeth arranged in a circle. The sea urchin lives near rocky shores, feeding on plants and decaying materials in the sea.

Sea Cucumbers The sea cucumber is a fleshy animal shaped something like a cucumber. The sea cucumber has spines that are very tiny. It can crawl along the ocean floor by moving the muscles of its body. The sea cucumber has five rows of tube feet. It uses the tube feet to attach itself to rocks. At one end of its body is the mouth, which is surrounded by **tentacles** (TEN tə kəlz). The tentacles are like tiny arms and can trap small animals.

Echinodermata

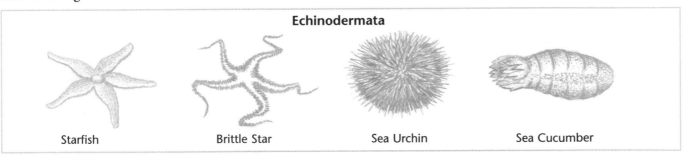

| Starfish | Brittle Star | Sea Urchin | Sea Cucumber |

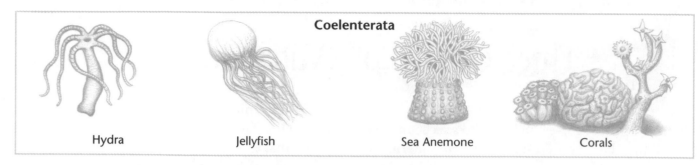

Coelenterata

Hydra   Jellyfish   Sea Anemone   Corals

Group 2: Coelenterata

Hydras, jellyfish, sea anemones, and corals all belong to a group called **Coelenterata** (si len tə RAH tə). The word *Coelenterata* means "hollow insides." All of these animals are hollow in the middle.

Hydra The hydra is a simple animal. Its body is a hollow tube sometimes only a quarter of an inch (half of a centimeter) long. The hydra's mouth is at one end of the tube. The other end of the tube is closed, and the animal uses this end as a foot. Between six and ten long tentacles grow out from around the mouth. The hydra is not a sea animal. It lives in fresh water. It clings to weeds, sticks, and stones.

Jellyfish The jellyfish is not a fish. This animal has a jellylike body in the shape of a bell. Its mouth is in the center of the underside of the bell. From the corners of its mouth extend arms that can grasp small animals. The bell of the jellyfish has many other arms around its edge. The jellyfish can swim slowly by <u>expanding</u> and <u>contracting</u> its bell. The swimming jellyfish looks like a balloon being filled with air and then being emptied of air over and over again. Jellyfish bells range in size from about 3 to 12 inches (8 to 30 centimeters) in diameter.

Sea Anemone The sea anemone (ə NEM ə nee) is so named because it looks like a many-colored, beautiful flower called an anemone. The sea anemone attaches itself to a rock or shell and stays there. Its mouth is surrounded by many tentacles. The sea anemone feeds on crabs and fish. It has a slimy disk, or foot, on which it can slide along. The sea anemone has the ability to regenerate a lost or injured part of its body.

Corals There are many different types of corals. Each type has a different shape, but each is covered by the same stony material. The stony coral is like the sea anemone. It remains attached to one spot and produces a cup of limestone material into which it can retreat. Millions of tiny corals live together. In warm seas, they build reefs of limestone. Coral jewelry is made from the colorful coral houses built by some of these tiny animals.

Group 3: Porifera

Many types of sponges belong to the group called **Porifera** (po RIF ə rə). The word *Porifera* means "pore bearer." Sponges have many pores, or holes. Sponges grow in different shapes. They may be dome-shaped or fan-shaped. The basket sponge, deadman's fingers, vase sponge, and bath sponge are named because of the way they look.

Sponges attach themselves to the ocean floor and do not move about. Like the starfish, brittle star, and sea anemone, sponges can regenerate. All sponges have one thing in common. They are made up of colonies of many tiny animals. Each cell of the sponge is able to feed itself and to get rid of its own waste.

The sponge has many whiplike parts, each called a **flagellum** (flə JEL əm). As each flagellum whips

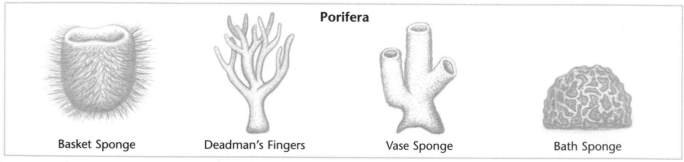

Porifera

Basket Sponge   Deadman's Fingers   Vase Sponge   Bath Sponge

about, it causes a flow of water. The movement of these whiplike parts causes water to enter the sponge through the pores, or openings, in its outer surface. Tiny plants and animals are thus brought in as food for the sponge.

A sponge has a framework that supports the soft mass of its living cells. This framework is the part that is sometimes still sold in stores as a natural sponge for cleaning. Most sponges provide living quarters for many other animals. Worms, shrimps, small crabs, and some small fish find homes in the canals and chambers of sponges. They also get food from the water that passes through the sponge's body.

COMPREHENSION

1. What happens if a starfish loses one of its arms?

   _____

2. What do all Coelenterata have in common?

   _____

3. What is a flagellum?

   _____

4. What does *Porifera* mean?

   _____

5. Where does the hydra live?

   _____

6. Go back to page 19 and reread the paragraph with a ✔ next to it. Underline the sentence that contains the main idea of the paragraph.

7. Underline the word that correctly completes each sentence.

   a. Milk can be drunk through a straw using

      _____.

      suction   tentacles   flagellum

   b. You are _____ your stomach when you hold it in.

      expanding   extending   contracting

   c. A tire is _____ when air is being pumped into it.

      regenerating   expanding   contracting

CRITICAL THINKING

1. What purpose might the skin of Echinodermata have?

   _____

   _____

2. Explain why it might be an advantage for brittle stars to have arms that break off easily.

   _____

   _____

3. The sand dollar has skin that is covered with short spines. It has tube feet and a mouth in the center of its underside. To which group does it probably belong? Explain.

   _____

   _____

A. Write the name of each of the three groups mentioned in the selection. Under each group name, write the names of the animals that belong to it.

Group 1 _____   Group 2 _____   Group 3 _____

_____   _____   _____

_____   _____   _____

_____   _____   _____

_____   _____   _____

B. Go back to the selection and reread the description of each type of Echinodermata. Complete the chart below by adding the characteristics of each animal. The first one is started for you.

Characteristic	Starfish	Brittle Star	Sea Urchin	Sea Cucumber
Body Structure	*central disk with five arms; mouth in center of underside of disk; tubes on underside of arms*			
Motion				

Reading-Writing Connection

Divide the items in your desk or backpack into at least two groups. What items belong in each group? How are the items in each group the same? How are the two groups different? On a separate sheet of paper, write a paragraph explaining how you classified the items.

Skill: Reading Decimals

BACKGROUND INFORMATION

The next selection, "How to Read Decimals," explains decimals, a way of writing numbers less than 1. The decimal system was developed in India more than 1,000 years ago. The English word *decimal* comes from the Latin word *decem*, meaning "ten." The decimal system is a base-ten system. That means that the value of each place to the left of the decimal point is ten times greater than the value of the place to the right of it. For example, 22 is ten times greater than 2.2, and 2.2 is ten times greater than .22.

SKILL FOCUS: Reading Decimals

A period in a number is called a **decimal point**. The digits to the left of the decimal point are whole numbers. The digits to the right of the decimal point are less than one.

The number *6.2* is an example of a decimal. The number *6* is to the left of the decimal point. So the 6 represents a whole number. The number *2* is to the right of the decimal point. So the *2* represents part of a whole number.

When reading a decimal, say the word *and* when you come to the decimal point. The number *6.2*, for example, is read as *six and two-tenths*. The number *33.3* is read as *thirty-three and three-tenths*.

▶ Look at each decimal below. On the lines, write words for the way you would say each number.

8.9 _____

_____

27.6 _____

_____

12.1 _____

_____

14.7 _____

_____

62.5 _____

_____

WORD CLUES

A **suffix** is a word part added to the end of a base word. In math, -*th* is a common suffix. When the suffix -*th* is added to a number word, such as *ten*, *hundred*, or *thousand*, the meaning of the word changes. A word with the suffix -*th* describes a value of less than 1.

Think about the difference between ten apples and a tenth of an apple. The suffix -*th* makes a big difference. Ten-tenths would make just one whole apple. If you have ten apples, you have a hundred times more than if you have just a tenth of an apple.

▶ Add the suffix -*th* to each number word. Write the new words on the lines.

ten _____

hundred _____

thousand _____

Strategy Tip

When reading "How to Read Decimals," pay special attention to the names of the place values to the right of the decimal point. Remember that the numbers in these places are always less than one.

How to Read Decimals

The following four place values all show whole numbers.

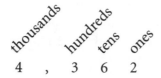

thousands hundreds tens ones
4   ,   3   6   2

There are also place values to the right of the ones place. These are called **decimal places.** A **decimal point**, or period, separates the ones place from the first decimal place. The places to the right of the decimal point show values of less than 1.

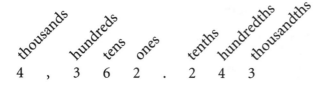

thousands hundreds tens ones tenths hundredths thousandths
4   ,   3   6   2   .   2   4   3

The first three places to the right of the decimal point are tenths, hundredths, and thousandths. A number in the tenths place is $\frac{1}{10}$ as large as the same number in the ones place.

Think about a dollar bill. It takes ten dimes to make a dollar. A dime is one-tenth of a dollar. One-tenth can be written as a decimal, 0.1, or as a fraction, $\frac{1}{10}$.

A number in the hundredths place is one-hundredth of the same number in the ones place. Again you can compare using decimal places to counting money. It takes 100 pennies to make a dollar. A penny is one-hundredth of a dollar. One-hundredth can be written as a decimal, 0.01, or as a fraction, $\frac{1}{100}$.

A number in the thousandths place is one-thousandth of the same number in the ones place. This is a very small part of a dollar. It is so small that there is no coin made for that value. One-thousandth can be written as a decimal, 0.001, or as a fraction, $\frac{1}{1,000}$.

If a number less than 1 is written as a decimal, a zero may be used to the left of the decimal point.

ones		tenths	hundredths	thousandths	
0	•	5			five-tenths
0	•	0	7		seven-hundredths
0	•	1	5		fifteen-hundredths
0	•	0	0	6	six-thousandths
0	•	0	1	7	seventeen-thousandths
0	•	5	7	2	five hundred seventy-two-thousandths

When reading a decimal number that has no whole numbers, ignore the zero. Read the number to the right of the decimal point as though it were a whole number. Then add the name of the place value. For example, 0.7 is read as *seven-tenths.*

Numbers that include digits on both sides of the decimal point are always read in two groups. Look at the following number.

376.4

First read the number to the left of the decimal point. Say the word *and* when you reach the decimal point. Then read the number to the right of the decimal point as though it were a whole number, and add the name of the place value. The number above should be read as *three hundred seventy-six and four-tenths.*

The same number could also be written as a whole number and a fraction. The number to the left of the decimal point is a whole number. The number to the right of the decimal point is a fraction. The 4 is in the tenths place, so the denominator of the fraction is 10. The number is written as follows.

$376\frac{4}{10}$

Look at the following number.

496.15

Read the number to the left of the decimal point first. Say the word *and* when you reach the decimal point. Then read the number to the right of the decimal point. Since the last digit is in the hundredths place, add the word *hundredths*. The number is read as *four hundred ninety-six and fifteen-hundredths*. The number is written as a whole number and a fraction as follows.

$$496\frac{15}{100}$$

Look at the following number.

537.207

It is read as *five hundred thirty-seven and two-hundred-seven-thousandths*.

Remember that the decimal point separates the whole numbers from the numbers that are less than 1. The numbers that appear to the right of the decimal point are always less than 1.

COMPREHENSION

1. What are the names, in order, of the first three places to the right of the decimal point?

   _____

2. What word is said when you reach the decimal point in a number?

   _____

3. If a dollar bill is one whole, what part of a dollar is a dime? A penny? Write each as a fraction and as a decimal.

   one dollar = _____

   one dime = _____ or _____ of a dollar

   one penny = _____ or _____ of a dollar

CRITICAL THINKING

1. Explain how a decimal and a fraction are the same.

   _____

   _____

2. Explain the function of zero in a decimal.

   _____

   _____

3. For each group of four decimals, circle the number with the largest value.

a. 0.5	0.07	0.01	0.05
b. 0.4	0.02	0.7	0.006
c. 0.6	0.03	0.3	0.087

A. Write each number in the correct column on the chart.

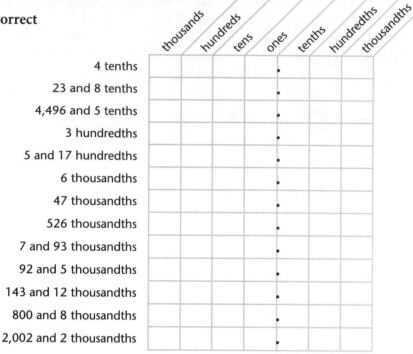

	thousands	hundreds	tens	ones	tenths	hundredths	thousandths
4 tenths				•			
23 and 8 tenths				•			
4,496 and 5 tenths				•			
3 hundredths				•			
5 and 17 hundredths				•			
6 thousandths				•			
47 thousandths				•			
526 thousandths				•			
7 and 93 thousandths				•			
92 and 5 thousandths				•			
143 and 12 thousandths				•			
800 and 8 thousandths				•			
2,002 and 2 thousandths				•			

B. Rewrite each decimal number as a fraction or as a whole number and a fraction.

0.6 _____   4.2 _____   423.001 _____   591.93 _____   0.42 _____

8.96 _____   1,492.013 _____   783.486 _____   0.157 _____   12.07 _____

C. Draw a line to match each decimal in the first column with the fraction in the second column that has the same value. Then match each fraction with its written-out number in the third column.

1.23	$1\frac{23}{1,000}$	12 and 3 tenths
.123	$12\frac{3}{100}$	1 and 203 thousandths
12.3	$1\frac{23}{100}$	1 and 23 hundredths
1.023	$1\frac{203}{1,000}$	12 and 3 thousandths
12.003	$\frac{123}{1,000}$	1 and 23 thousandths
12.03	$12\frac{3}{1,000}$	123 thousandths
1.203	$12\frac{3}{10}$	12 and 3 hundredths

Reading-Writing Connection

On a separate sheet of paper, write a paragraph describing three occasions when you had to read or use decimals.

Skill: Silent Letters

When a one-syllable word contains two vowels, one of which is a final *e*, the final *e* is usually **silent**. When two vowels come together in a one-syllable word, the second vowel is usually silent.

A. Cross out the silent vowel in each word below.

1. hole	5. boat	9. tribe
2. sea	6. shore	10. fire
3. line	7. coast	11. gleam
4. reach	8. home	12. coat

Consonants, as well as vowels, can be silent. Below are some cases when a consonant is silent.

k before *n,* as in *knee*

w before *r,* as in *write*

c before *k,* as in *kick*

b after *m,* as in *lamb*

gh after *au, ou,* or *i,* as in *caught, thought,* and *light*

t in the middle of a one-syllable word, as in *hatch*

d in the middle of a one-syllable word, as in *hedge*

B. Say each word below to yourself. Cross out the silent vowels and consonants.

1. wrap	12. night	23. truck
2. file	13. patch	24. beak
3. badge	14. toad	25. fudge
4. meat	15. wreck	26. dime
5. bought	16. nine	27. latch
6. limb	17. watch	28. steam
7. cute	18. train	29. stone
8. crack	19. struck	30. taught
9. hose	20. tape	
10. fight	21. knot	
11. dough	22. high	

Skill: Main Idea

The **main idea** is the most important idea in a paragraph. Often the sentence that has the main idea is the first or last sentence. You can find the main idea sentence if you ask yourself, "Which sentence states what the paragraph is about?"

Read the following paragraphs about woodpeckers. Below each one are four sentences that appear in the paragraph. Underline the sentence that is the main idea of the paragraph.

1. Several kinds of woodpeckers live in North America. The flicker, a brown-backed woodpecker with red markings, is fairly common. The little downy woodpecker, another common woodpecker, usually lives in orchards. The acorn woodpecker lives in the forests of western North America.

   a. The little downy woodpecker, another common woodpecker, usually lives in orchards.

   b. The acorn woodpecker lives in the forests of western North America.

   c. Several kinds of woodpeckers live in North America.

   d. The flicker, a brown-backed woodpecker with red markings, is fairly common.

2. The red-headed woodpecker is one of the most common kinds of woodpeckers. It lives in the central and eastern parts of the United States. It looks for grubs by boring holes in the bark of trees. It doesn't live on grubs alone, however. It also eats fruit, especially berries. This woodpecker is about 10 inches long. It is a very colorful bird. Its head, neck, and throat are red. Its back, tail, and upper wings are black. Its lower wings and under sections are white.

   a. It is a very colorful bird.

   b. Its back, tail, and upper wings are black.

   c. This woodpecker is about 10 inches long.

   d. The red-headed woodpecker is one of the most common kinds of woodpeckers.

3. The woodpecker's bill is sharp and strong. With it, the woodpecker chisels holes in trees where food will be. Its tongue is long and sharp. The woodpecker uses its tongue to spear insects, insect eggs, and grubs. One kind of woodpecker sucks sap from trees. This woodpecker has a brush on the end of its tongue to collect the sap. The woodpecker's bill and tongue help it get food.

   a. The woodpecker's bill is sharp and strong.

   b. The woodpecker's bill and tongue help it get food.

   c. One kind of woodpecker sucks sap from trees.

   d. The woodpecker uses its tongue to spear insects, insect eggs, and grubs.

4. Woodpeckers build their nests in holes in trees. Sometimes they dig a new hole in a live tree. Sometimes they find a hole in a dead tree. The female looks the hole over carefully while the male is digging into it. After the female decides that the hole is suitable, she helps the male with the digging. Finally they line the hole with sawdust and wood chips to make a nest.

   a. Woodpeckers build their nests in holes in trees.

   b. Sometimes they dig a new hole in a live tree.

   c. Finally they line the hole with sawdust and wood chips to make a nest.

   d. After the female decides that the hole is suitable, she helps the male with the digging.

How can you find information about a subject you are studying or want to know more about? You can use **reference books** in a library or at home. You need to know what kind of information each reference book contains in order to select the one you need. It is easy to locate information if you use the right reference books.

Suppose a friend is going to give you a sitar, but you are not certain what a sitar is. You can find the word *sitar* in a **dictionary**. You know that a dictionary defines words. It also shows how words are spelled, pronounced, and divided into syllables, and what parts of speech they are. Some dictionary entries also include a picture.

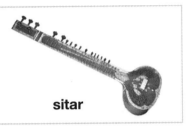

si·tar (si tär') *n*. a musical instrument of India with a long neck, and strings that vibrate along with those being played. *See the picture.*

sitar

Once you find out what the word *sitar* means, suppose you want to learn more about the instrument. You might want to know what kinds of sounds it makes, where it was developed, or how it is played. What reference book could you use? You may already know that an **encyclopedia** is a book or set of books containing articles on many subjects. An encyclopedia would provide the kind of information you want.

Sitar, *sih TAHR*, is a stringed instrument that originated in India or Persia. It is used in the classical music of northern India, Pakistan, and Bangladesh. The sitar has a long, broad neck made of wood and a pear-shaped body made from a large gourd. It has 7 main strings, which the musician plucks with a wire pick worn on the right index finger. It also has 12 or more *sympathetic strings*. These strings vibrate when the main strings are played. Adjustable metal strips called *frets* are attached to the neck of the instrument. They serve as fingering guides for the left hand.

The sitar probably was developed in the A.D. 1200s. It reached its present form during the 1800s and 1900s. It serves chiefly as a solo instrument, usually accompanied by a drum called a *tabla* and a lute called a *tambura* that produces a *drone* (continuous pitch). A sitarist improvises within a certain melodic framework called a *raga* and a metrical framework called a *tala*. The instrument has become more familiar in the West since the 1960s. The Beatles and other rock groups have used it in their music.

Valerie Woodring Goertzen

While reading the encyclopedia, you may become curious about India, the country where the sitar was first developed. You may wonder how many people live there today. To find out, you would use an **almanac**. Although an encyclopedia may give the population of India, the figure may not be current. An almanac is a book with the most up-to-date information on many different subjects. Because it is printed every year, its information is more current than information found in other references. An almanac contains weather reports, facts about the United States and other countries, current events, sports facts, world records, and interesting information about people.

Area and Population by Country, Mid-2000

Country	Area (in sq. km)	Population	Country	Area (in sq. km)	Population
Afghanistan	647,500	25,888,797	Hungary	90,030	10,138,844
Albania	28,750	3,490,435	Iceland	103,000	276,365
Algeria	2,381,740	31,193,917	India	3,287,590	1,014,003,817
Angola	1,246,700	10,145,267	Indonesia	1,919,440	224,784,210
Antigua and Barbuda	440	66,464	Iran	1,648,000	65,619,636
Argentina	2,766,870	36,955,182	Iraq	437,072	22,675,617

A. Write the name of the correct reference book next to the kind of information it contains.

Choose from *dictionary*, *encyclopedia*, and *almanac*.

1. book with important facts printed yearly _____

2. book with meanings, spellings, and pronunciations of words _____

3. book with articles on many different subjects _____

B. Complete each situation by writing *dictionary*, *encyclopedia*, or *almanac* on the line.

1. Sergio wants to go mountain climbing with his older sister and brother. They tell him that he may go along if he has enough stamina. Sergio doesn't know what the word

   stamina means. Before he goes on the trip, he should use the _____.

2. Angela heard someone say that there was a "baby boom" last year—that more babies were born last year than in quite a few years before. To check if this information is

   correct, Angela should use the _____.

3. Jamal and his mother are moving from Phoenix, Arizona, to Baltimore, Maryland. Jamal wants to learn about Baltimore's history. To find such facts about his new city,

   Jamal should use the _____.

4. José is writing a letter to his grandfather. José wants to write about his new pet parakeet, but he is not sure how to spell the word *parakeet*. He needs to check

   the _____.

5. May Ling's class is going to visit Mount Vernon, the home of George Washington. Before the visit, May Ling wants to find out more about the first president and his

   life at Mount Vernon. To find this information, she should use the _____.

6. Yousef is studying a floor plan of his new school. He doesn't recognize the word *gymnasium* on one of the rooms. He looks up the word and sees that it is pronounced (jim nā′zē əm). He realizes he will play basketball in that room. Yousef found this

   information in the _____.

7. Mr. Gordon's class is studying weather. The students are interested in learning up-to-date information about the places and dates of the highest and lowest temperatures, as well as the greatest rainfalls and snowfalls. The students should

   look in the _____.

8. Victor is making a graph comparing the number of votes the candidates for governor of his state received in each of the last four elections. To find the

   information he needs, he should use the _____.

9. Abby is copying a report she has written. She is almost at the end of a line on her paper and finds that she can fit only part of the word *manufacturing* on the line. To

   find out where to divide the word into syllables, she should use the _____.

Skill: Hard and Soft c and g

The consonant c has two sounds, **soft c** as in *cent* and **hard c** as in *can*. The consonant g has two sounds, **soft g** as in *gem* and **hard g** as in *goose*.

When you come to a new word that contains either c or g, there is a rule that can tell you which sound to use in pronouncing the word.

A. Write an answer to each of the questions in the headings. Then fill in the words necessary to complete the rule.

	What vowel comes after c?	*Does c have the hard or soft sound?*
1. cape	_____	_____
2. common	_____	_____
3. curve	_____	_____

RULE: Usually c has the _____ sound when it is followed by the vowel

_____, _____, or _____.

B. Write an answer to each of the questions in the headings. Then fill in the words necessary to complete the rule.

	What vowel comes after c?	*Does c have the hard or soft sound?*
1. center	_____	_____
2. cider	_____	_____
3. cycle	_____	_____

RULE: Usually c has the _____ sound when it is followed by the vowel

_____, _____, or _____.

C. Write an answer to each of the questions in the headings. Then fill in the words necessary to complete the rule.

	What vowel comes after g?	*Does g have the hard or soft sound?*
1. gate	_____	_____
2. goblet	_____	_____
3. gulf	_____	_____

RULE: Usually g has the _____ sound when it is followed by the vowel

_____, _____, or _____.

D. Write an answer to each of the questions in the headings. Then fill in the words necessary to complete the rule.

	What vowel comes after g?	*Does g have the hard or soft sound?*
1. gentle	_____	_____
2. giant	_____	_____
3. gym	_____	_____

RULE: Usually *g* has the _____ sound when it is followed by the vowel

_____, _____, or _____.

E. Now make a rule that can be used with both *c* and *g*.

RULE: Usually *c* and *g* have the hard sound when followed by the vowel _____,

_____, or _____ and the soft sound when followed

by the vowel _____, _____, or _____.

This rule has a few exceptions, as in *get, girl,* and *give.* In most cases, however, the vowel letter following *c* or *g* will show what sound to use in pronouncing a new word.

F. Below are some words that contain either *c* or *g*. Say each word to yourself. Decide which sound the *c* or *g* has in each word. Write *hard* or *soft* on the line.

1. general	_____	**8.** garden	_____	**15.** rage	_____
2. gush	_____	**9.** gypsy	_____	**16.** cash	_____
3. civilian	_____	**10.** oxygen	_____	**17.** gunpowder	_____
4. curtain	_____	**11.** citizen	_____	**18.** giraffe	_____
5. cymbals	_____	**12.** certain	_____	**19.** cinder	_____
6. cabin	_____	**13.** gull	_____	**20.** captain	_____
7. compare	_____	**14.** cite	_____	**21.** germ	_____

G. Read the story below. Underline every word that has a hard or soft *c*, or a hard or soft *g*. If the letter has the hard sound, write *h* above it. If the letter has the soft sound, write *s* above it.

The Magic Boat of Lake Geneva

Once there was a strange boat on Lake Geneva. It had no engine. White swans with silken cables in their beaks gently pulled it.

This was a magic boat. A fairy princess stood in it. Her hair was golden yellow. Her head covering was set with gems. She wore a gown of many colors.

Whenever the boat came to the shore, corn and wheat began to sprout, and cypress trees came up in all the gardens.

Very few of the country people ever saw the boat. When one of them happened to catch a view of it, his purse was filled with gold. He never had to go to work again.

Skill: Prefixes and Suffixes

A prefix is a word part that is added to the beginning of a word to change its meaning.

A. Circle the prefix in each of the words below.

discover	enlarge	supermarket	renew	unhappy	preview
depart	subway	misspell	dislike	redo	indoors

A suffix is a word part that is added to the end of a word to change its meaning.

B. Circle the suffix in each of the words below.

statement	swiftly	national	quickest	straighten	helpful
sweetness	clearly	loudness	darken	hopeless	teacher

C. Write one of the prefixes below on the line next to each word to make a new word with a meaning that agrees with the given definition.

Prefix	Meaning
un-	not
re-	back, again
in-	in, toward
pre-	before

1. _____wanted   not wanted

2. _____sew   to sew again

3. _____usual   not usual

4. _____heat   to heat before

5. _____patch   to patch again

6. _____land   toward land

D. Write one of the suffixes below on the line next to each word to make a new word with a meaning that agrees with the given definition.

Suffix	Meaning
-er	one who does
-ful	full of
-en	made of, to become
-ness	quality or state of

1. farm_____   one who farms

2. near_____   quality of being near

3. wonder_____   full of wonder

4. sweet_____   to make sweet

5. joy_____   full of joy

6. sing_____   one who sings

Skill: Reading a Recipe

A **recipe** is a set of instructions for making something to eat or drink. The ingredients tell what and how much to use. They are listed first. The steps to follow in preparing the food are next. It is important to follow the steps in the right order. If you read the directions carefully, you can follow any recipe.

Study the following recipe. Notice the abbreviations in the list of ingredients and the metric conversions in parentheses.

SEAFOOD AND SPAGHETTI

1 doz uncooked shrimp, peeled and deveined
½ lb (.225 kg) sea scallops
40 small to medium mussels, rinsed well
1 onion, sliced thin
1 garlic clove, chopped fine
3 T (45 mL) olive oil
1 lemon, sliced thin

1 large can of Italian plum tomatoes, mashed and drained
½ can tomato paste
½ c (.12 L) clam juice
1 t (5 mL) dried basil
1 T (15 mL) oregano
½ t (2.5 mL) pepper
1 t (5 mL) salt
1 lb (.45 kg) spaghetti

1. Cook onion and garlic in oil in large pot.
2. When onion is soft, add lemon, tomatoes, tomato paste, basil, oregano, salt, and pepper. Simmer for 25 minutes, stirring occasionally.
3. Add clam juice and simmer until sauce thickens, about 15–20 minues.
4. Cook spaghetti according to directions on package.
5. Add shrimp, scallops, and mussels to sauce. Cover and cook on high heat until mussels open, about 5 minutes. Lower heat and simmer uncovered until spaghetti is done.
6. Drain the spaghetti. Empty into large bowl. Pour sauce and seafood over spaghetti. Serve immediately.

SERVES 4–6 PEOPLE

A. Below are the steps to follow for the seafood and spaghetti recipe. Write 1 in front of the first step to follow, 2 in front of the next step to follow and so on.

_____ Add the lemon, tomatoes, tomato paste, basil, oregano, salt, and pepper, and simmer for 25 minutes.

_____ Add the shrimp, scallops, and mussels, and cook on high heat until mussels open.

_____ Cook the spaghetti according to directions on package.

_____ Cook onion and garlic in oil in large pot.

_____ Empty the drained spaghetti into large bowl and pour sauce and seafood over spaghetti.

_____ Add clam juice and simmer until sauce thickens.

B. Fill in the circle next to the answer to each question.

1. What kinds of seafood are used in this recipe?
   ○ shrimp, scallops, mussels
   ○ onion, garlic, oil
   ○ scallops, mussels, lemon
   ○ shrimp, scallops, garlic

2. What do you need to do to the onion before you cook it?
   ○ Cut it in half.
   ○ Slice it thin.
   ○ Chop it fine.
   ○ Shred it.

3. Once the onion is soft, about how long does the sauce simmer before the seafood is added?
   ○ 25 minutes
   ○ 15–20 minutes
   ○ 20–30 minutes
   ○ 40–45 minutes

4. Why do you think you have to stir the sauce occasionally while it is cooking?
   ○ so it doesn't stick to the bottom of the pot
   ○ so all of the ingredients will cook for the same amount of time
   ○ so you won't forget that you have something cooking on the stove
   ○ so all of the ingredients will cook evenly

5. Why doesn't the recipe explain how to cook the spaghetti?
   ○ There probably wasn't enough room in the recipe.
   ○ Everybody already knows how to cook spaghetti.
   ○ Everybody cooks it to a different degree of softness.
   ○ The directions for cooking the spaghetti are on the spaghetti package.

6. How do you know that you should cook the shrimp without their shells?
   ○ The recipe calls for frozen shrimp.
   ○ The recipe calls for uncooked shrimp.
   ○ The recipe calls for peeled shrimp, so you must remove the shells.
   ○ The recipe calls for covering and cooking the shrimp on high heat.

7. Why do you think the recipe says to cover the pot once the mussels are in?
   ○ The cover keeps the heat in the pot, which makes the mussel shells open.
   ○ The cover allows the heat to escape from the pot, which keeps the mussel shells closed.
   ○ The cover keeps the mussels in the pot so that they do not jump out.
   ○ The cover keeps the flavor of the mussels in the pot.

8. The recipe serves four to six people. What does that mean?
   ○ Depending on the size of the shrimp and scallops, it will serve about 46 people.
   ○ It serves four adults or six children.
   ○ It will be enough for six people who will eat four servings.
   ○ Depending on how large the portions are, it will be enough for four, five, or six people.

9. How could you prepare this recipe for two or three people?
   ○ Use half the amount of each ingredient.
   ○ Double the ingredients.
   ○ Triple the ingredients.
   ○ Use one-third of the amount of each ingredient.

Challenges

LESSON 11

Skill: Conflict and Resolution

BACKGROUND INFORMATION

"Slow-to-Let-Go" is based on the childhood of a great leader of the Sioux (soo) people. The Native Americans known as the Sioux, or Lakota (lə KOH tə), lived in the upper Great Plains. Their lands included parts of what are now Nebraska, Minnesota, and the Dakotas. Skilled hunters, the Sioux depended on buffalo for their food, clothing, and shelter.

SKILL FOCUS: Conflict and Resolution

In most stories, the main character has a goal or a problem. The struggle to achieve this goal or solve this problem is called the story's **conflict**.

There are three main types of conflict.

1. A character might have a **conflict with self.** That means that he or she struggles with inner feelings.

2. A character might have a **conflict with another character**.

3. In some stories, there is a **conflict with an outside force**, such as nature, society, or a dangerous animal.

By the end of a story, the main character succeeds or fails in solving the conflict. The way a conflict is settled is called the **resolution**.

▸ Think about each conflict on the chart below. Then write the type of conflict each character faces and a possible resolution.

CONTEXT CLUES: Comparisons

Some context clues are **comparisons**. The word *like* or *as* usually appears in front of a comparison. Notice the clue to the meaning of *slithered* in the following sentences.

> *A long line of Lakota hunters* **slithered** *silently through the waving prairie grass in what is now South Dakota. As they moved like rattlesnakes, their feet whispered over the ground.*

If you don't know the meaning of *slithered*, the phrase *moved like rattlesnakes* can help you. The movement of the hunters is compared to the movement of snakes, using the word *like*.

▸ Circle the comparison that helps you figure out the meaning of *stampeding* in the following sentence.

> *The buffaloes were* **stampeding** *now, like a crowd of people running from a brush fire.*

In "Slow-to-Let-Go," the words *pierced, honorable,* and *sprint* are underlined. Look for comparison context clues that help show their meanings.

> #### Strategy Tip
>
> As you read "Slow-to-Let-Go," think about the conflicts the main character faces. Look for the resolution to each one.

Conflict	Type of Conflict	Resolution
Bill's mom says he cannot buy a car even though he has a driver's license.		
Eric has to sing a solo, but he has stage fright.		
A tornado approaches Ellie's farmhouse in Oklahoma.		

Slow-to-Let-Go

A long line of Lakota hunters slithered silently through the waving prairie grass in what is now South Dakota. As they moved like rattlesnakes, their feet whispered over the ground. In the front were the best hunters. In the rear was a ten-year-old boy.

A herd of grazing buffaloes moved slowly down the plain toward the hunters. The hunters spread out and quietly crept toward the buffaloes. When they had almost reached the herd, they froze, arrows ready. They waited, hidden by the tall grass.

A lick of wind brought the animals' scent to the hunters. The boy watched closely through the crooked branches of a bush. Big and shaggy-haired, the buffaloes passed some of the lead hunters. Some of them were taller than his father, Jumping Bull. They would soon be nearing the boy.

Suddenly the quiet of the prairie was broken by the roar of pounding hoofs. The animals had smelled the hunters and started to run. Hunters jumped from cover, sighted their arrows, and let the arrows fly. The buffaloes were stampeding now, like a crowd of people running from a brush fire. The ground shook beneath their hoofs as the animals rumbled toward the boy.

The boy fitted an arrow to his bow. He picked out a red-eyed bull running toward him. He aimed just above and behind the animal's front shoulder. The arrow shot from his bow and <u>pierced</u> the galloping animal. Although the arrow stabbed the buffalo like a bolt of lightning, it kept running, pushed on by others, thundering close behind.

The boy grabbed another arrow and ran after the bull. The herd swung away, but his buffalo slowed. The herd had left the wounded buffalo behind. The boy ran hard, seeking a second shot. Suddenly the great animal stopped. Its legs folded. The heavy beast fell down, rolled twice, then lay still.

It was dead. Slow-to-Let-Go had killed his first buffalo with only one shot.

Slow-to-Let-Go was given his name when he was a baby. Given food, he studied it, turning it this way and that before eating it, even when he was hungry. Given a rattle, he never wanted to let it go. He was careful about everything he did. Therefore he learned from everything he did. He was careful and not afraid to try new things.

A Lakota man must be a good hunter. Slow-to-Let-Go proved his skill by killing his first buffalo at

age ten. Above all, a Lakota boy must grow to be a brave warrior. When he was only 14, Slow-to-Let-Go became a warrior. On that day in 1851 when he became a warrior, he earned a new name. Under this name he became one of the most famous Native American leaders in American history.

It was one of the long, golden days of summer. The young boy watched his father and the other warriors ride out of the village. The village was camping for the summer on the heights above the Grand River in South Dakota. A few miles away was a creek. There the warriors would join Lakotas from other villages for a war party against the Crows.

Whenever Slow-to-Let-Go talked of going on these war parties, his family told him that he was not old enough. They said he was not yet a man. His father always agreed.

This time, Slow-to-Let-Go would try something instead of talk. When the men were out of sight, Slow-to-Let-Go jumped onto his horse and followed them. No one noticed him. He caught up with the men at the creek and rode to where his father stood.

"What are you doing here?" asked Jumping Bull.

"I am going, too," said Slow-to-Let-Go.

"Warriors are not made in 14 winters, my son."

Slow-to-Let-Go said nothing but looked calmly at his father.

"Warriors must be brave," Jumping Bull told him.

Slow-to-Let-Go nodded. "That is why I am here," he said, "to show I am brave."

Jumping Bull looked at his only son. Then he raised his hand. "My son will ride with us," he said.

He stepped closer to the boy. "You are not old enough to carry a warrior's arrows," he said, "but you can prove your courage with this." He handed his son a stick with a feather on it.

To the Lakotas and other Plains Indians, war was a testing ground to prove a warrior's courage. One way to show courage was to "count coup" (coo). A warrior counted coup by touching an enemy with a coup stick. When a fight began, the bravest warriors raced ahead to touch the enemy with their coup sticks. Getting away without being killed was more <u>honorable</u> than killing the enemy. These fast and brave warriors were considered as noble as a king.

"Your horse is fast," said Jumping Bull. "You must show that your heart is brave."

The Lakotas rode for several days, but the scouts found no sign of the Crows. One day, the party made camp behind a low hill. A scout called down from the hilltop. There was something far off—perhaps only a dust cloud or some buffaloes.

Others joined the scout. They watched until they were sure. An enemy party about the size of the Lakota party was coming at a gallop. The men grabbed their weapons and ran for their horses.

Slow-to-Let-Go was quickly painted bright yellow from head to foot. His gray horse was painted red. He grabbed his coup stick and leaped onto his horse. The wind whistled past him as he thundered down the hill and across the plain.

The Crows stopped suddenly. They began to turn their horses back. They were going to run! The Lakotas bellowed with anger as they chased the Crows across the plain.

Slow-to-Let-Go thumped his heels against his horse's flanks, causing it to <u>sprint</u> like a jackrabbit. The Lakotas were catching up with the fleeing Crows. Slow-to-Let-Go had the honor of being the first into battle.

Suddenly Slow-to-Let-Go could see the Crows' faces as they looked back. The enemy drew their bows and arrows. They turned, aiming for the leaders of the Lakota charge.

Very quickly, Slow-to-Let-Go was among the Crows. He caught up with a Crow warrior who drew his bow and turned to shoot at the Lakotas. The boy cut his horse closer to the enemies. He lashed out with his coup stick. The stick struck the Crow's arm just as he shot his arrow. The arrow flew into the ground.

The running battle ended in a few minutes. The Lakotas gathered the horses and weapons they had won and turned for home. When they got to the village, Jumping Bull painted his own horse black. This was the sign of victory and honor. Then he put his son on the horse and led him around the village.

"Hear me!" Jumping Bull cried. "My son has counted coup in his first battle! He was first to strike the enemy! My son is brave!

"From this day my son is a warrior. Today I give him a new name. This name is Sitting Bull!"

1. What happened to the buffalo after Slow-to-Let-Go shot it with his arrow?

   _____

   _____

2. What did Slow-to-Let-Go prove when he killed his first buffalo?

   _____

   _____

3. After Slow-to-Let-Go proved his skill as a hunter, what else did he want to prove?

   _____

   _____

4. How did Slow-to-Let-Go prove his courage as a warrior?

   _____

   _____

5. What new name did Jumping Bull give his son when his son became a warrior?

   _____

6. Where do the events in this story take place?

   _____

7. Write the word below that could be used in place of the underlined word or phrase in each sentence.

   pierced   sprinted   honorable

   a. The lion ran fast for a short distance.

      _____

   b. The noble factory owner helped to find new jobs for the laid-off workers.

      _____

   c. The cook stabbed the steak with a knife to check if it was done.

      _____

CRITICAL THINKING

1. Describe how Slow-to-Let-Go lived up to his name when he hunted his first buffalo.

   _____

   _____

2. Do you think Slow-to-Let-Go's new name, Sitting Bull, fits him? Explain.

   _____

   _____

3. Explain why Jumping Bull was proud of his son.

   _____

   _____

4. Do you think Slow-to-Let-Go was brave when he counted coup? Explain.

   _____

   _____

Think about the conflicts that Slow-to-Let-Go faces and how he resolves them. Write your answers on the lines provided.

1. What are Slow-to-Let-Go's goals? _____

   _____

2. What conflict does Slow-to-Let Go face at age ten? _____

   _____

3. How does Slow-to-Let-Go resolve the conflict he faces on the buffalo hunt? _____

   _____

4. What does Slow-to-Let-Go learn as a result of his experiences during the buffalo hunt? _____

   _____

5. Think about the three kinds of conflict. Which kind of conflict does Slow-to-Let-Go face on his first hunt?

   _____

6. With whom does Slow-to-Let-Go come into conflict during his first battle? _____

   _____

7. How does Slow-to-Let-Go resolve the conflict of his first battle? _____

   _____

8. What does Slow-to-Let-Go learn as a result of his first battle? _____

   _____

9. Think about the three kinds of conflict. Which type of conflict does Slow-to-Let-Go face

   during his first battle? _____

   _____

10. How does Slow-to-Let-Go change as a result of the conflicts in the story? _____

    _____

Reading-Writing Connection

Think about Slow-to-Let-Go's character. Do you think that he would be a good leader today? On a separate sheet of paper, write a paragraph explaining why he would or would not make a good leader today. Consider the kinds of conflicts he would have to resolve.

Skill: Cause and Effect

BACKGROUND INFORMATION

"The Red Tail Angels," is about the first African American pilots of World War II, the Tuskegee Airmen. Beginning with the American Revolution, African Americans have fought in our nation's wars. However they once had to fight in all-black units. By the time the United States entered World War II, in 1941, blacks and whites still could not fight together. The Tuskegee Airmen would finally change that situation.

SKILL FOCUS: Cause and Effect

When one event makes another event happen, the process is called cause and effect. A **cause** is any reason, situation, or condition that makes something happen. An **effect** is the result of a cause.

Sometimes a cause can have more than one effect. The first chart shows how one cause resulted in two effects. The second chart shows an effect that is the result of more than one cause.

Cause

The official policy of the military was to limit opportunities for African Americans.

Effect 1

The Coast Guard and Marines took no African Americans in 1941.

Effect 2

In the Navy, African Americans could work only at kitchen jobs.

- -

Cause 1

Black leaders pressured lawmakers to let African Americans become pilots.

Cause 2

One African American sued the government for the right to fly.

Effect

The Army announced that it would open its first pilot-training school for African Americans.

▶ Read the following sentences. Underline the sentences that are causes once. Underline the sentence that is an effect twice.

The Army would not send the Tuskegee Airmen into combat at first. White officials were prejudiced against the pilots. They also questioned their flying ability.

CONTEXT CLUES: Definitions

Some reading selections include the **definitions** of new words. A word's meaning is usually given after the new word.

Read the following sentences. Look for the definition of the underlined word.

Early in 1942, the Tuskegee Airmen became the 99th <u>Squadron</u>. A squadron is eight or more airplanes that fly and fight together.

If you don't know the meaning of *squadron* in the first sentence, you can learn it by reading its definition in the next sentence.

▶ Read the following sentences. Circle the definition that tells you the meaning of *stereotypes*.

These officers tended to believe <u>stereotypes</u> about the races. A stereotype is a fixed view about a group of people that does not allow for individual differences.

When reading "The Red Tail Angels," use definitions to learn the meanings of the underlined words *segregation*, *bigotry*, and *casualty*.

Strategy Tip

As you read "The Red Tail Angels," look for cause-and-effect relationships. Recognizing causes and effects will help you understand the ideas in the selection.

The Red Tail Angels

ON JULY 2, 1943, German fighter planes surrounded 16 American bombers. The bombers had just attacked the enemy over Italy. Now the Americans were returning to their base in North Africa. Would they make it?

The swift German fighters closed in on the big American bombers. Before the Germans could fire, however, American fighter planes dived down on them. The lead German plane exploded in a ball of flames. The other German fighters were under attack, too. The crews of the American bombers sighed in relief. The Tuskegee (tus KEE jee) Airmen, America's first African American combat pilots, were on the job!

Before the Tuskegee Airmen

Today there are many African American combat pilots. Before the Tuskegee Airmen, however, no blacks had ever flown in combat. As in many areas of American life, African Americans had limited opportunities in the armed services.

Segregation (SEG rə GAY shən) was the official policy of the military. Segregation means separation of the races. The Coast Guard and Marines, for example, took no African Americans in 1941. In the Navy, African Americans could work only at kitchen jobs. The Army accepted black and white volunteers, but soldiers of different races fought in separate units. During World War II, the Air Force was part of the Army.

As early as 1939, African American leaders asked President Franklin Roosevelt to **desegregate** (dee SEG rə GAYT) the army. They wanted black soldiers to fight in the same units that white soldiers did. Most white army leaders, however, were against such a plan. These officers tended to believe stereotypes about the races. A stereotype is a fixed view about a group of people that does not allow for individual differences. The white military leaders thought that black and white soldiers would not get along in combat.

A Breakthrough at Tuskegee

As the war effort geared up, the demand for pilots grew. Some African Americans already knew how to fly. Others were ready and able to learn. They wanted to serve their country as pilots, but their country would not let them.

Black leaders pressured lawmakers to let African Americans fly. One African American pilot sued the government for the right to fly. In July of 1941, a breakthrough came. The Army announced that it would open its first pilot-training school for blacks.

The school would be at Tuskegee Institute in Tuskegee, Alabama. Tuskegee is a well-known college founded by Booker T. Washington. Since 1881, African Americans had studied science and technology there. Now the school would also be training pilots.

Hundreds of African American men applied to enter the first flight-training classes. Many had college degrees from top universities. Their test scores on a qualifying test were so high that white officers suspected them of cheating. Forced to take a second test, they scored just as high.

Getting Into the Fight

Late in 1941, the first class of Tuskegee Airmen got their wings. More trainees were arriving at the Alabama airfield every month. They were all eager to defend their country.

Many of the Tuskegee Airmen were college graduates. They received high scores on the tests they took to qualify for flight training.

The Army, however, would not send the Tuskegee Airmen into combat. White military officials were **prejudiced** (PREJ ə dist) against the Tuskegee pilots. They had a low opinion of the pilots just because of their race and would not judge them fairly. They also questioned their flying ability. Frustrated, the Tuskegee Airmen felt like second-class citizens.

Things began to change when First Lady Eleanor Roosevelt, the wife of President Franklin D. Roosevelt, visited Tuskegee in 1941. She took a test flight with one of the Tuskegee Airmen. The visit created good publicity (pub LISS ə tee) for the airmen. Newspapers and magazines took photos and wrote about the flight. People wanted to know where and when the pilots would be fighting.

Early in 1942, the Tuskegee Airmen became the 99th Squadron. A squadron is a group of eight or more airplanes that fly and fight together. The all-black unit was under the leadership of Lieutenant Colonel Benjamin O. Davis, Jr. Davis would later become the first African American major general.

Fighting in Tunisia

In 1942, the 99th Squadron was posted to Tunisia (too NEE zhə) in North Africa. The Americans and the countries fighting with them were called the Allies. The Allies were fighting against the Germans and Italians in North Africa.

The Tuskegee Airmen were ordered to stop the enemy from delivering supplies to its troops. They had to bomb enemy trucks, tanks, and railroads. They had to blow up bridges and fuel supplies.

It was a very dangerous assignment, or job. The airmen had to fly deep into enemy territory to reach their targets. They also had to fly low, only a few hundred feet above the ground. That was the only way to hit small targets. Deadly enemy guns pounded away at them all the time.

The 99th Squadron did an amazing job. They blew up hundreds of supply trains and trucks. Without supplies, the enemy could not fight. Unfortunately the Tuskegee Airmen got little praise at first. There was still much bigotry for them to overcome. Bigotry means narrow-mindedness.

We think of the Tuskegee Airmen as pilots. For every pilot, however, there were ten soldiers

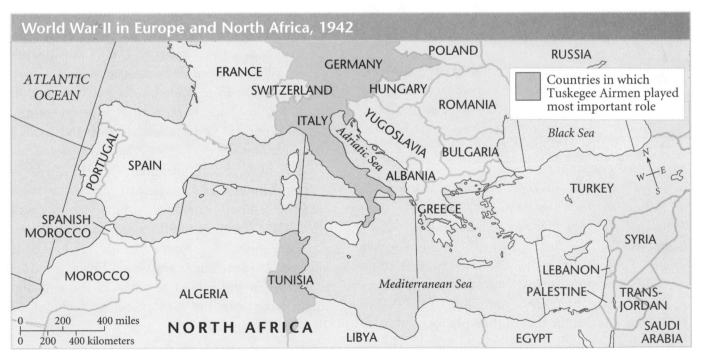

In World War II, Germany and Italy tried to gain control of countries in North Africa. The Tuskegee Airmen played an important role in stopping them.

supporting him on the ground. Some were airplane mechanics. Others maintained airfields. There were office workers, doctors, and cooks. Because the squadron was segregated, all of these support people were African Americans, too.

A New Assignment in Europe

Late in 1943, the Tuskegee Airmen were transferred to Italy. There the 99th Squadron joined the 332nd Squadron. This larger, all-black unit was given an important new assignment.

The African American pilots of the 332nd Squadron called themselves "the Red Tail Angels."

The United States was bombing enemy targets in Europe. Bombers, however, were large and slow airplanes. They could not maneuver easily. They flew out to their targets, dropped their bombs, and flew home. Along the way, they were easy targets for enemy fighter planes.

The job of the Tuskegee Airmen was to escort, or follow along to protect, the bombers. When German fighter planes attacked, the 332nd Squadron had to fight them off. It was another challenging assignment. The Tuskegee Airmen would be going up against Germany's best pilots.

To identify themselves, the pilots of the 332nd Squadron painted the tails of their planes bright red. They called themselves "the Red Tail Angels." To the enemy, the red tails said, "Try to get us!" When an American bomber pilot saw a red tail, however, he knew he would be protected.

The air fighting over Europe was fierce. In just ten months, pilots of the 332nd Squadron shot 136 enemy planes out of the air. Altogether the 332nd squadron flew 1,578 missions. They won 150 Distinguished Flying Crosses and 744 air medals. They received more medals than any other pilots in the war.

The Tuskegee Airmen had another impressive record. In all, they escorted thousands of bombers during the war. Yet not one of those bombers was ever shot down. No other fighter group in the Air Force could match that.

The news of the Red Tails' skill got around. Their bravery became well known. When white bomber pilots flew a mission, they asked for the Tuskegee Airmen to protect them.

A Job Well Done

By the end of the war, the Tuskegee Airmen had nothing left to prove. They had fought long and hard and well. They were as good as any other pilots the military had ever seen. They had shot down hundreds of airplanes and destroyed more on the ground. They had disabled countless enemy trains, trucks, and tanks. They had sunk 40 enemy boats. Once they even sank a German destroyer, using just a machine gun!

Like all pilots in World War II, the Tuskegee Airmen had a high casualty rate. Casualties are people killed or wounded in battle. Some 992 men had graduated from pilot training at Tuskegee. Of them, 150 lost their lives in combat or on training flights. Another 32 were shot down and held as prisoners of war.

The brave accomplishments of the Tuskegee Airmen helped President Truman make a decision. In 1948, Truman ordered the military to **integrate** (IN tə GRAYT) black soldiers and white soldiers in the same units. Segregation would no longer be allowed. African Americans would finally get equal treatment in the armed services. In the end, that might have been the greatest achievement of the Tuskegee Airmen.

1. How was the Army different for African Americans in 1941 than it is today?

_____

_____

2. When did the United States open its first training school for African American pilots?

_____

_____

3. Where did the Tuskegee Airmen first fight during World War II?

_____

_____

4. How did First Lady Eleanor Roosevelt help the Tuskegee Airmen?

_____

_____

5. In 1942, what did the Tuskegee Airmen have to do on their first assignment in the war?

_____

_____

6. In 1943, what assignment was given to the Tuskegee Airmen in Europe?

_____

_____

7. Explain why the Tuskegee Airmen were sometimes called "the Red Tails."

_____

_____

8. In all, how many African American pilots were trained at Tuskegee?

_____

_____

9. What important order did President Truman sign after World War II?

_____

_____

10. Write the letter of the correct meaning on the line next to each word.

_____ segregation   **a.** someone killed or wounded

_____ bigotry   **b.** separation of the races

_____ casualty   **c.** narrow-mindedness

CRITICAL THINKING

1. Explain why you think the Tuskegee Airmen got little praise at first for their work in North Africa.

_____

_____

2. Discuss why you think white bomber pilots began to ask for the Tuskegee Airmen as their escorts.

_____

_____

3. State facts to show that the Tuskegee Airmen were involved in very dangerous missions.

_____

_____

4. Explain how the actions of the Tuskegee Airmen helped overcome bigotry in the armed forces.

_____

_____

SKILL FOCUS: CAUSE AND EFFECT

A. Write one or more causes of each of the following effects.

1. **Cause:** _____

   Effect: There were no African American fighter pilots before 1941.

2. **Cause:** _____

   Cause: _____

   Effect: The American public learned about the Tuskegee Airmen and wanted them
   to join the fighting.

3. **Cause:** _____

   Cause: _____

   Effect: Disrupting the enemy supply lines in North Africa was a dangerous assignment.

B. Write one or more effects of each of the following causes.

1. **Cause:** In Tunisia, the Tuskegee Airmen destroyed enemy trains, trucks,
   and fuel supplies.

   Effect: _____

2. **Cause:** Bombers were big and slow.

   Cause: They could not maneuver easily.

   Effect: _____

3. **Cause:** To protect the bombers, the Tuskegee Airmen fought bravely and well.

   Effect: _____

4. **Cause:** President Truman was much impressed by the Tuskegee Airmen.

   Effect: _____

Reading-Writing Connection

You are asked to give a short speech to honor the Tuskegee Airmen. On a separate sheet
of paper, write the speech that you would give.

Skill: Following Directions

BACKGROUND INFORMATION

In "What Are Memories Made Of?" you will learn what scientists have discovered about how the brain stores memories. Without memory, life as we know it would vanish. We would have no names, no friends, no science, and no beliefs. To know anything at all, we depend on memory. Unlocking the secrets of memory is a great challenge facing science today.

SKILL FOCUS: Following Directions

Following directions is an important skill. To conduct a science experiment, for example, you must follow the steps of the directions exactly.

Directions for science experiments are set up in a special form. That way, different people can repeat them and compare results. The directions for many experiments are divided into the following five parts.

1. **Problem** The problem is often a question that you should be able to answer at the end of the experiment.

2. **Aim** The aim tells what will be done during the experiment.

3. **Materials** Materials are the objects or equipment needed to perform the experiment.

4. **Procedure** The procedure lists the steps that must be carried out to complete the experiment.

5. **Observations or Conclusions** Based on the outcome of the experiment, you should be able to make certain observations or draw conclusions.

Use the following steps to help you read a selection with directions for an experiment.

1. Read the paragraphs that explain the ideas on which the experiment is based. Be sure that you understand the ideas.

2. Read the five parts of the directions carefully. Be sure that you understand all the scientific words.

3. If there are any pictures or diagrams, study them carefully. Be sure to read the captions and labels.

4. Reread the Problem, Aim, Materials, Procedure, and Observations or Conclusions. Be sure you understand what to do to begin the experiment.

▶ Recall a science experiment you did in school recently. On the lines below, write the problem and aim of the experiment.

Problem: _____

_____

Aim: _____

_____

CONTEXT CLUES: Appositive Phrases

Some context clues are **appositive phrases**. An appositive phrase explains the meaning of a word that comes before it. It is usually set off from the word by commas or dashes, and often by the word *or*.

Read the sentence below. What appositive phrase explains the meaning of the underlined word?

The human brain, however, is far more __fallible__, or likely to make mistakes.

If you don't know the meaning of *fallible*, the appositive phrase *or likely to make mistakes* can help you figure it out.

▶ Circle the appositive phrase that explains the meaning of *reinforced* in the following sentence.

When information is repeated, these chemical connections are __reinforced__, or made stronger.

As you read the next selection, look for the underlined words *fibers*, *activated*, and *distinguish*. Use appositive phrases to help you figure out their meanings.

Strategy Tip

After you read "What Are Memories Made Of?" study the directions for the experiment on page 49. Use the four steps on this page to help you understand the experiment.

What Are Memories Made Of?

HAVE YOU EVER CRAMMED FOR A TEST and then forgotten some of the facts a day later? Can you recall the first day of kindergarten perfectly but remember nothing from last Thursday? If so, your memory is working just the way it should.

Nerve Cells and Chemicals

Your brain has more than 100 billion nerve cells, called **neurons** (NUR ahnz). A neuron is made up of a cell body, plus <u>fibers</u>, or threads, that stretch outward from it. One fiber, the **axon** (AKS ahn), carries signals away from the cell. Other nerve fibers, called **dendrites** (DEN dreyets), carry signals toward the cell.

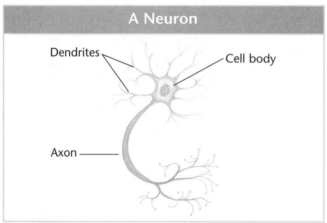

A Neuron

Dendrites — Cell body

Axon ———

The axon of one neuron carries a message to a dendrite attached to another neuron.

When information about the world comes in through your five senses, the brain goes into action. Chemical messengers flood across certain neurons, making new connections between them.

When information is repeated, these chemical connections are reinforced, or made stronger. When that happens, the signals pass more quickly. This is how your brain forms memories. A memory is the result of chemical changes in your neurons.

Experiments have shown the importance of chemicals in memory. In one experiment, a group of laboratory rats were given extra doses of a certain brain chemical. These rats learned a path through a maze to find food very quickly.

A second group of rats had a normal amount of the brain chemical. They had a much harder time learning the route. A third group of rats was totally denied the brain chemical. They were unable to learn or remember the route at all.

Not Like a Computer

People sometimes compare the brain to a computer. A computer organizes information neatly in separate files. Nothing is ever forgotten. The human brain, however, is far more fallible, or likely to make mistakes. That is because the brain scatters its memories in many different places. One group of nerve cells is <u>activated</u>, or put to use, when we say certain types of words. Other groups let us remember different types of words. One group of neurons helps us see an object's color. Another group lets us remember the same object's use.

The brain is more creative than a computer. Often one piece of information can trigger many different groups of neurons. The smell of a certain food, for example, might cause you to remember a party where you ate that food. In your mind, you might also see the people at the party, or hear the music, or remember the gifts.

Studying the Brain

Scientists use special machines to take pictures of the brain. At present, however, these machines cannot <u>distinguish</u>, or tell apart, the regions of the brain where different memories lie. They are too slow to catch the flash of chemicals racing across the brain's neurons. Much of what we know about memory, therefore, comes from patients with brain injuries.

When one part of the brain is injured, a person may lose part of his or her memory. By noting where the injury is and what kind of memory loss occurs, scientists can figure out what that part of the brain does.

✔ One part of the brain is called the hippocampus (HIP ə CAMP əs). When it is damaged, patients cannot form new memories. They can remember everything that happened before their injury, but nothing that happens after the injury. Scientists think that the hippocampus is the "hub" of memory. That means that all new experiences must pass through the hippocampus in order to become memories.

Another small section of the brain is called the amygdala (ə MIG də lə). When it is damaged, patients cannot recall emotions. That is, they cannot remember how they feel or have felt.

How's Your Memory?

We all know how complicated our memories are. Even perfectly normal brains can play tricks on people. We might easily remember some useless bit of information from an old TV commercial. At the same time, we might forget a key fact or an important name that we really need to remember.

The Three Types of Memory

There are three major types of memory. **Short-term memory** lasts for only 15 or 20 seconds. That's just long enough to keep a telephone number in your mind as you dial it. Short-term memory is very handy. It keeps our brains from getting clogged up with information we no longer need. After all, you wouldn't want to remember every phone number you ever dialed for the rest of your life.

Working memory is a special type of short-term memory that lasts a little longer. Usually, it lasts as long as you need it. You might use it to work a math problem or to talk with friends. After the problem is solved or the conversation is over, you have a general memory of the experience, but can forget many of the details.

Long-term memory lasts a long time, perhaps for your entire lifetime. Your knowledge of language, important events in your life, and motor skills such as riding a bike are all part of your long-term memory.

EXPERIMENT

PROBLEM
What information do we tend to remember in everyday life and what information do we tend to forget?

AIM
In this experiment, you will see how short-term and long-term memory affect learning.

MATERIALS
Two sets of 20 index cards, numbered from 1 to 20, with the name of a common object written in the middle of each card. (Use words such as cat, tree, button, sneakers, book, and so on.)

PROCEDURE
1. Choose a partner.
2. Read the list of words to your partner. Read the words in order from 1 to 20, at the rate of about one word per second.
3. Immediately after the last word is read, ask your partner to write down as many of the words as he or she can remember.
4. Check your partner's list. Compare the words that your partner wrote with the words on the index cards.
5. Note the numbers written on the cards of the words your partner remembered. Did your partner tend to remember the first words on the list? Did he or she tend to remember the last words on the list? What about the words in the middle?
6. Change roles with your partner and perform the experiment again. Make a second set of index cards with different words. Again, use words for common objects.

OBSERVATIONS OR CONCLUSIONS
Most people tend to remember the first words on the list. That's because people are able to rehearse and practice these words for a longer time.

Most people also tend to remember the last words on the list. These words are still in their short-term memory, so they can recall them easily.

Words in the middle of the list are usually the most difficult to remember. These are no longer in short-term memory and have not made it into long-term memory.

SCIENCE

1. What is a neuron?

   _____

2. How are axons and dendrites alike and different?

   _____

   _____

   _____

3. Find the paragraph in the selection that has a ✓ next to it. Underline the sentence that tells the paragraph's main idea.

4. The first part of the selection describes an experiment with rats and a brain chemical. Summarize the results of the experiment.

   _____

   _____

   _____

5. What happens to some patients who receive an injury to the hippocampus of the brain?

   _____

   _____

6. About how long does short-term memory last?

   _____

   _____

7. Write the letter of the correct meaning on the line next to each word.

   _____ activated   **a.** threads

   _____ distinguish **b.** tell apart

   _____ fibers   **c.** put into action

CRITICAL THINKING

1. After performing an experiment, why is it important to list your observations?

   _____

   _____

2. Explain why you can probably remember an important day from several years ago better than you can remember the details of a conversation you had in class last week.

   _____

   _____

3. Tell why the author says that the human brain is more creative than a computer.

   _____

   _____

4. Conclude why it is important for people to have both short-term memory and long-term memory.

   _____

   _____

1. Write a summary of the experiment on page 49. Do not look back. Then check your summary by rereading the experiment. Correct your work.

_____

_____

_____

_____

_____

2. Sometimes the brain has trouble remembering two kinds of information at the same time, such as color and language. Read the following experiment that demonstrates this idea. Then complete the experiment below. On the lines, write the Materials, Procedure, and Observations or Conclusions for the experiment you have

just read. The Problem and Aim are filled in.

Using crayons, write the words blue, red, yellow, green, pink, purple, black, *and* brown *on a sheet of paper. Write each word twice, in mixed-up order. Use a blue crayon to write the word* blue, *a red crayon to write* red, *and so on.*

On another sheet of paper, make a similar list, but do not match the color word and the color of the crayon you use to write it. For example, use a purple crayon to write the word yellow, *a red crayon to write* blue, *and so on. With a stopwatch, time how long it takes a partner to read each list. Note how many mistakes, if any, the partner makes while reading each list.*

EXPERIMENT

PROBLEM
How does color affect the brain's ability to process language?

AIM
In this experiment, you will learn that the brain has trouble sometimes processing two different kinds of information: language and color.

MATERIALS

_____

PROCEDURE

1. _____

_____

_____

2. _____

_____

_____

3. _____

_____

_____

4. _____

_____

_____

OBSERVATIONS OR CONCLUSIONS

_____

_____

_____

_____

_____

Reading-Writing Connection
On a separate sheet of paper, write a paragraph to describe one of your favorite memories. Include as many details as you can about what you saw, heard, smelled, touched, and tasted.

Skill: Reading Roman Numerals

BACKGROUND INFORMATION

In "The Roman Numeral System," you will learn how to read Roman numerals. Roman numerals are a different system, or language, of numbers than Arabic numbers, which we use every day. The Roman numerals I, V, and X, for example, have the same meaning as the Arabic numbers 1, 5, and 10. Roman numerals were used in Europe until the 1200s. Then Europeans switched to Arabic numbers. Arabic numbers are easier to add, subtract, multiply, and divide than Roman numerals are.

SKILL FOCUS: Reading Roman Numerals

Today, Arabic numbers have replaced **Roman numerals.** However, you will still see Roman numerals from time to time. Roman numerals are used in outlines, for example. The numerals I, II, III, and so on mark the main sections of an outline.

People sometimes use Roman numerals when they want a number to look dramatic. For example, the thirty-sixth Super Bowl was called Super Bowl XXXVI, as well as Super Bowl 36. You may also notice Roman numerals on the cornerstones of buildings. There they show the date when the building was completed.

Roman numerals are read differently from Arabic numbers. When reading Arabic numbers, the position of each digit—its place value—helps you read the number. The Roman numeral system is not based on place value. To read Roman numerals, you have to add or subtract the values of the symbols. To figure out the meaning of XXV, for example, you have to add two 10s and one 5.

▶ Use the chart below to help you add the values of each symbol in the next column. Write the Arabic number for each Roman numeral.

Roman	Arabic
I	1
V	5
X	10

XX _____

XV _____

VII _____

XXVI _____

XVIII _____

WORD CLUES: Reading Roman Numerals

In "The Roman Numeral System," look for the words *Roman numerals, symbol,* and *Arabic numbers.* Be sure that you understand the different symbols used in the Roman and Arabic numeral systems.

Strategy Tip

When reading "The Roman Numeral System," think about the value of each Roman numeral. Remember to read the Roman numerals from left to right. Also follow the rules in the selection for adding and subtracting the values of the symbols in each numeral.

THE ROMAN NUMERAL SYSTEM

Roman numerals (NOO mər əlz) were first used thousands of years ago. People started to use numerals because they needed to count and record numbers. The first **symbol**, or written sign, representing a number that the Romans used was a vertical line. It became the Roman symbol for the number one.

$$I = 1$$

Other numbers were written using the symbol for one.

$$III = 3$$
$$IIIIIIIII = 9$$

As you can imagine, it would take time and space to write the number 38 using just the symbol for the number one. It also would take time to read the number 38. That is why new symbols were invented for numbers larger than three. These numerals made reading larger numbers easier.

$$V = 5$$
$$X = 10$$

Roman symbols can be used over and over again. For example, in the Roman numeral XXXII, the symbol X appears three times and the symbol I appears twice. Unlike **Arabic numbers**, the value of a Roman symbol does not depend on its place. For example, in the number XXXII, each X stands for the value of 10 and each I for the value of 1.

To read a Roman number, you must add the values of the symbols. In the following example, the symbol with the largest value is at the far left. Then comes the symbol with the next largest value, and so on. The symbol that stands for the smallest value is at the far right.

$$XVI = 10 + 5 + 1 = 16$$

If a smaller-value symbol appears to the left of a larger value, you need to use another step before you add. The smaller value to the left is subtracted from the larger value to its right. Then all the values of the symbols are added.

XIV
Step 1: $IV = 5 - 1 = 4$
Step 2: $XIV = 10 + 4 = 14$
XXIX
Step 1: $IX = 10 - 1 = 9$
Step 2: $XXIX = 10 + 10 + 9 = 29$

In the Roman numeral system, four or more of the same symbols are never used in a row. For example, instead of IIII, the numeral for four is written as five minus one. Instead of IIIIIIIII, the numeral for nine is written as 10 minus 1.

$$IV = 5 - 1 = 4$$
$$IX = 10 - 1 = 9$$

Here are the steps for reading Roman numerals.

1. Check whether the symbols are in order from greatest value to least value.

2. If the symbols are in that order, add the values of the symbols.

3. If the symbols are not in that order, subtract the symbol for the smaller number from the symbol to its right. Then add the values.

As the Romans faced the challenge of counting and recording larger and larger numbers, they invented other symbols. Here are some.

$$L = 50$$
$$C = 100$$
$$D = 500$$
$$M = 1,000$$
$$\overline{V} = 5,000$$
$$\overline{X} = 10,000$$

The following examples show how these numerals are used to make larger numbers.

$$LXVII = 67$$
$$XLIX = 49$$
$$XC = 90$$
$$DCCX = 710$$
$$MMCM = 2,900$$
$$\overline{V}MCCXVII = 6,217$$
$$M\overline{V}CX = 4,110$$
$$\overline{XXX}CC = 30,200$$

1. When were Roman numerals first used?

   _____

2. What was the first symbol the Romans used, and what was its value?

   _____

3. Why were new symbols invented for numbers larger than 3?

   _____

4. In a Roman numeral, when are the values of the symbols subtracted?

   _____

5. What is the Roman symbol for 10,000?

   _____

6. What are three steps for reading a Roman numeral?

   _____

   _____

   _____

   _____

   _____

CRITICAL THINKING

1. Name the symbol that is lacking in the Roman system.

   _____

2. Explain what would happen to the value of the numeral if the order of the symbols in a Roman numeral were changed.

   _____

3. Tell why you think that four or more of the same symbol are never used in a row in the Roman system.

   _____

4. Explain how you think the Romans used their number system in daily life.

   _____

SKILL FOCUS: READING ROMAN NUMERALS

A. Give the value for each Roman numeral below. Because the symbols are in order from the largest value to the smallest, you will only have to add the values.

1. I	= _____		5. XV	= _____
2. III	= _____		6. XVI	= _____
3. V	= _____		7. XXX	= _____
4. X	= _____		8. XXVIII	= _____

9. L = _____ **17.** CC = _____

10. LX = _____ **18.** CCCLXXXVIII = _____

11. LXV = _____ **19.** D = _____

12. LXX = _____ **20.** DXXVI = _____

13. C = _____ **21.** MMLXVIII = _____

14. CL = _____ **22.** MMM = _____

15. CX = _____ **23.** $\overline{V}$ = _____

16. CLXV = _____ **24.** $\overline{XX}$ = _____

B. Give the value of each Roman numeral below. You will sometimes have to subtract before you add.

1. XIV = _____ **6.** DLXIV = _____

2. XXXIX = _____ **7.** MCM = _____

3. LXVI = _____ **8.** MCML = _____

4. CDXIX = _____ **9.** $M\overline{V}CCIX$ = _____

5. XLVII = _____ **10.** $M\overline{X}CMXCIX$ = _____

C. Give the Roman numeral for each Arabic number below.

1. 18 = _____ **13.** 9,500 = _____

2. 188 = _____ **14.** 1,800 = _____

3. 15,000 = _____ **15.** 1,425 = _____

4. 220 = _____ **16.** 26 = _____

5. 550 = _____ **17.** 8 = _____

6. 250 = _____ **18.** 13 = _____

7. 1,700 = _____ **19.** 5,250 = _____

8. 4,000 = _____ **20.** 17,000 = _____

9. 75 = _____ **21.** 650 = _____

10. 59 = _____ **22.** 29 = _____

11. 400 = _____ **23.** 68 = _____

12. 48 = _____ **24.** 72 = _____

Reading-Writing Connection

Find two places where you can see Roman numerals. On a separate sheet of paper, write a paragraph describing where you found each numeral, and explain what each one means.

A **prefix** is a word part that is added to the beginning of a word to change its meaning. Four common prefixes and their meanings are given below.

Prefix	Meaning
mis-	wrong or badly
out-	away from or better than
under-	below or not enough
over-	above or too much

A. Change the meaning of each word below by adding a prefix. Write the new word in the first column. Write the meaning of the new word in the second column.

1. over + head = _____   _____

2. mis + treat = _____   _____

3. under + fed = _____   _____

4. out + run = _____   _____

B. Use a prefix from the list above to make each phrase below into one word. Write the new word on the line.

1. to eat too much   _____   3. to behave badly   _____

2. not sold for enough   _____   4. to do better than   _____

A **suffix** is a word part that is added to the end of a word to change its meaning. Three common suffixes are *-ion, -ition,* and *-ation.* All three suffixes mean the act of, the result of, or the state of.

C. Add one of the suffixes to each word below to make a new word. If the word ends with *e,* cross out the *e* before adding the suffix. If you are unsure of the spelling, use a dictionary.

1. direct _____   3. inform _____   5. oppose _____

2. define _____   4. locate _____   6. declare _____

D. Use one of the words above to complete each sentence below.

1. Squanto gave the Pilgrims valuable _____ about planting corn.

2. The Pilgrims wanted a _____ in Virginia for their settlement.

3. When the Pilgrims landed, they faced no _____ from the Native Americans.

4. The _____ of Independence was adopted on July 4, 1776.

5. The _____ of a pilgrim is "a person who travels about."

LESSON 16

Skill: Prefixes and Suffixes

A. Read the prefixes and their meanings in the box below. Then add one of the prefixes to each word below to make a new word.

Prefix	Meaning
dis-	away or opposite of
super-	bigger, greater, or larger
trans-	over, across, or beyond

1. _____appear = opposite of appear
2. _____market = big market
3. _____place = move away from its place
4. _____atlantic = across the Atlantic
5. _____highway = large highway
6. _____port = to carry across

B. Use one of the words above to complete each sentence below.

1. A _____ contains many kinds of food.
2. Large jet planes make many _____ flights every day.
3. Cargo ships _____ many of this country's products to other countries.
4. The magician made the rabbit _____ from view.

C. Read the suffixes and their meanings in the box below. Then add one of the suffixes to each word below to make a new word.

Suffix	Meaning	Suffix	Meaning
-al	belonging to, or the act of	-able	capable of doing something
-ment	state of being, act	-ist	one who does a certain thing
-y	full of, or covered with	-less	without

1. move _____ = state of being in motion
2. art _____ = one who does artwork
3. water _____ = without water
4. tropic _____ = belonging to the tropics
5. accept _____ = capable of being accepted
6. length _____ = having length

D. Use one of the words above to complete each sentence below.

1. The 800-page book seemed _____ to Jane.
2. The _____ of the Earth around the Sun takes one year.
3. John's homework was messy. His teacher said it was not _____.
4. The soil of most deserts is almost _____.

Skill: Fact and Opinion

Do you know the difference between a fact and an opinion? A **fact** is a statement that can be proved. An **opinion** is a statement of belief or feeling that cannot be proved.

Fact: Mexico is our neighbor to the south.

Opinion: Mexico has the greatest art treasures in the world.

Read this letter written by a student to the editor of a newspaper. Think about which statements are facts and which are opinions.

Dear Editor:

Last week our local art museum held an exhibit called "Art from Around the World." Hundreds of people saw the show. Your own paper praised the museum for its fine work. I saw the show and thought it was very good. However, I feel that the country of Mexico was neglected.

Mexico is our neighbor to the south. It is a large country with a long history. The ancient cultures of the Maya, Toltec, and Aztec peoples are important in Mexican history. I think the art of these people is some of the most interesting in the world. It seems to me that some of this art should have been included in the exhibit.

When Spanish settlers came to Mexico, they brought with them their own style of art and design. Their influence is still seen today in Mexico, as well as in the United States. Yet, the exhibit did not include any art from the Spanish colonial period.

Some of the greatest painters in Mexico worked after the Mexican revolution. Artists, such as José Orozco and Diego River, painted colorful murals to show the story of the revolution. These murals were painted on the walls of public buildings. In my opinion, photos of these murals also should have been shown.

Today Mexico is home to many young artists. The exhibit at the art museum included only two of their paintings. I believe that the talented young artists of Mexico deserve more attention. Their work is some of the most interesting new art being produced today!

I hope that the next time the museum has an exhibit of world art, they will not forget Mexico. The artists of ancient Mexico, old Mexico, and modern-day Mexico have given me much pleasure. It's time that other people in our city had a chance to enjoy them!

Paul Ramon

Read each of the following statements. Decide if it is a fact or an opinion. Then on the line next to each statement, write *F* for fact or *O* for opinion.

_____ 1. Your own paper praised the museum for its fine work.

_____ 2. However, I feel that the country of Mexico was neglected.

_____ 3. Mexico is a large country with a long history.

_____ 4. I think the art of these people is some of the most interesting in the world.

_____ 5. It seems to me that some of this art should have been included in the exhibit.

_____ 6. Yet, the exhibit did not include any art from the Spanish colonial period.

_____ 7. These murals were painted on the walls of public buildings.

_____ 8. In my opinion, photos of these murals also should have been shown.

_____ 9. Today Mexico is home to many young artists.

_____ 10. I believe that the talented young artists of Mexico deserve more attention.

Skill: Main Idea—Stated or Unstated

When you read a textbook or reference book for information, you often find the **main idea** of each paragraph **stated** in a sentence. The supporting details, which give more information about the main idea, are found in the rest of the paragraph. Sometimes, however, the main idea of a paragraph is **unstated**. You will need to infer the main idea yourself. To do this, think about the supporting details. Then think of a sentence that summarizes the supporting details.

As you read each paragraph below, decide whether the main idea is stated or unstated.

1. Monkeys are small, lively mammals that rank high among the most intelligent animals. Scientists classify monkeys in the highest order of mammals. This order is the primates. Because monkeys are so intelligent, they can learn many tricks. Their liveliness makes them favorites of zoo visitors.

2. The New World monkeys, one of two major groups of monkeys, live in Central and South America. The Old World monkeys live in Asia and Africa. The nostrils of New World monkeys are spaced more widely apart than those of the Old World monkeys. Most kinds of New World monkeys have 36 teeth. All Old World monkeys have 32 teeth. Some New World monkeys can hold things with their tail, but no Old World monkeys can.

3. Many people believe that apes, which include chimpanzees, gibbons, gorillas and orangutans, are like monkeys. However, monkeys and apes differ in several ways. For instance, apes are more intelligent than monkeys. Apes do not have tails, while most monkeys do. Most species of apes are larger than monkeys.

4. Monkeys use their long arms and legs to help them climb and leap. They grasp the branches of trees with their hands and feet. Most types of monkeys have a long tail that helps them keep their balance. While moving through trees, some monkeys use their tail to grasp branches.

5. Almost from the moment of birth, a baby monkey hangs on to its mother by grasping her fur. The infant clings to its mother's chest at first. Later it rides on her back. Until the baby can travel safely on its own, its mother carries it. A baby monkey feeds on its mother's milk. Depending on the species, a baby monkey receives its mother's milk for a few weeks up to two years.

A. For each paragraph above, if the main idea is stated, write *stated* on the line. If the main idea is unstated, choose a main idea from below and write its letter on the line.

a. Baby monkeys are easy to care for.

b. A monkey's body enables it to move easily through trees.

c. New World monkeys are smaller than Old World monkeys.

d. The two major groups of monkeys are the New World monkeys and the Old World monkeys.

e. Baby monkeys are very dependent on their mothers.

Paragraph 1 _____   Paragraph 3 _____   Paragraph 5 _____

Paragraph 2 _____   Paragraph 4 _____

B. Go back to each paragraph that has a stated main idea. Underline the sentence with the main idea.

Skill: Reading the White Pages

What can you do if you want to call a friend on the phone but you can't remember his or her number? The best thing to do is to look up your friend's telephone number in the **white pages** of the phone book. Names in the white pages are listed alphabetically, last names first. After a person's last name, the first name or initial, the address, and the phone number are given.

You can quickly find the name you are looking for by using the **guide words** at the top of each page. The guide words give the last name of the first entry on the page and the last entry on the page. Guide words help you to know if the name you are looking for is on that page of the phone book.

Study the listings below from the white pages of a phone book. Notice that the names of businesses that are initials only are listed alphabetically before the other names.

B — BARNES	
B & B SPORTING GOODS 11 Forest Av 555-3600	Barbour J 4099 Afton Ct 555-8268
BJ'S BICYCLE SHOP 232 Hampton Rd 555-0880	Barbour J 841 Juniper Av 555-4811
BWI AIRLINES –	Barbour William K 189 Kings Point Rd . . . 555-6831
Reservations & Information 555-3000	Barclay Ken 5993 Oakwood St 555-4218
Bach Richard J 16 Ridge Rd 555-7942	Barclay Margaret 135 Roanoke St 555-7263
Baddleman Mrs P 2 Stoney Hill La 555-1024	Barclay Scott D 127 Mountain Rd 555-3181
Bader John R 406 Walter St 555-7033	Bark Edith 345 Ocean Blvd 555-5217
Ball Lee & Connie 208 Bark 555-3794	Barkas Maurice 289 Hollycrest La 555-6950
Banks I 29 Piedmont Dr 555-1132	Barker Eugene J 100 Centershore Rd 555-1937
BARBARA'S BARGAIN STORE	Barker Harry C 2904 Cobb St 555-2287
20 Forest Av 555-5299	Barker Harry Q 824 Treehouse Ct 555-8604
BARBER – See Also BARBOUR	Barker L 2938 Village St 555-8352
Barber C L 47 Spruce Hollow Rd 555-3583	Barker Zachary 99 W. Fordham St 555-5733
Barber George 24 Shoreline 555-4552	BARKER'S PHARMACY 406 Main St 555-0288
Barber Gina 28 Woodstock 555-4921	Barkley Kam C 835 Laurelwood Dr 555-3501
Barber Stuart 113 Brookville 555-9844	Barksdale William L 77 Darnell Dr 555-1493
Barbera Julio 239 Huntington Rd 555-0384	BARNACLE BILL'S RESTAURANT
BARBI-LEE DANCE STUDIO	92 Dune Rd 555-3400
24 Annandale Rd 555-9456	Barnes A 4273 Yardley Blvd 555-5441
Barbini Sonia 609 Meadowlark La 555-1891	Barnes Arthur 14 Rolling Woods L 555-6635
BARBIZON HOTEL 400 Main St 555-6666	Barnes Brooke 4273 Yardley Blvd 555-5441
Barbour Alice 192 Huntington Rd 555-1276	

A. Use the phone listings above to answer each question.

1. **a.** How many businesses are listed?

_____

    b. What are the names of two of them?

_____

_____

_____

2. Which five last names have more than one listing?

_____

_____

3. You have to speak to Edith Bark. What is her address and phone number?

_____

4. What is the phone number of the Harry Barker who lives on Cobb Street?

   _____

5. What is the address of a Mr. Barnes whose phone number is 555-6635?

   _____

6. a. How can you find the phone number of your friend Alissa Barclay if you don't know her mother's or father's first name but you do know that she lives on Roanoke Street?

   _____

   _____

   b. Whose name is Alissa's phone number listed under?

   _____

7. You want to call your soccer coach, James Barber, but you're not sure of the spelling of his last name. He lives on Afton Court. What is his phone number?

   _____

8. Which two people named Barnes do you think are related? Why?

   _____

9. a. If Terry Barber were listed in the phone book, whose name would be right before hers?

   _____

   b. Whose name would be right after hers?

   _____

10. Why isn't the Briarwood School listed on this page?

   _____

B. Use the following information to make a sample phone book page on the lines below. List the names in alphabetical order, last name first. The first entry is done for you.

Adriano Rodriguez	58 Cres Rd	555-3506
ROD TOOL CO	35 Second Av	555-7630
Freddie Rodriguez	470 West Rd	555-1034
A Rodriguez	85 Audubon Rd	555-7724
Barbara Rizner	7812 Ridge Ter	555-8614
James O Rodney	280 Bart Dr	555-0385
Fernando Rodriguez	7 Steve Rd	555-5539
Al Rodriguez	5401 Water St	555-4823

RIZNER – ROF

Rizner Barbara   7812 Ridge Ter   555-8614 _____

_____

_____

_____

_____

_____

_____

_____

Finding Your Way

LESSON 20

Skill: Character

BACKGROUND INFORMATION

In "Ana's Project," Ana sets up a nonprofit organization to help people in need. Nonprofit organizations do not try to earn money. They are supported by contributions from people. Many people volunteer to work for these organizations. In the United States, there are thousands of nonprofit organizations working to achieve worthwhile goals. The Girl Scouts provides special programs for people. The American Heart Association raises money for medical research that will help save people's lives. Some nonprofit organizations help people during floods and emergencies. Others work to save animals and the environment.

SKILL FOCUS: Character

Characters are the people in a story or novel. A story can have a few or many characters. Usually there is one main character, who plays the major part in the story's action. The other characters are not as important as the main character.

The main character usually wants to achieve a goal or solve a problem. Most of the character's actions are directed toward achieving the goal or solving the problem. Often the character changes as he or she faces challenges in the story.

As you read a story, use the following questions to better understand the main character.

• Who is the main character?

• What is the main character's goal or problem?

• What does the main character do to achieve the goal or solve the problem?

• How does the main character change by the end of the story?

▌ Think of a story you know well. On the Idea Web in the next column, describe the story's main character.

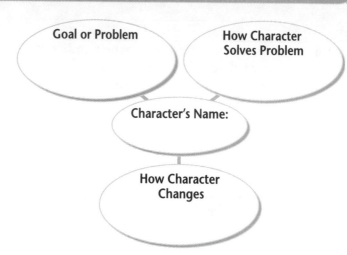

CONTEXT CLUES: Appositives

An **appositive** is a word or phrase that explains the meaning of another word in the same sentence. It is often set off by commas and starts with the word *or*.

▌ Look for the appositive that explains the meaning of the underlined word in the following sentence.

*The next week, Ana and Mrs. Eisen thought of a **strategy**, or plan, to solve the problem.*

If you don't know the meaning of *strategy*, the appositive *or plan* will help you.

▌ Read the sentences below. Circle the appositive that explains the term *nonprofit organization*.

*First, he helped her set up a **nonprofit organization**, a company that does not make a profit.*

As you read, use appositives to figure out the meanings of *donated*, *drive*, and *online*.

> ### Strategy Tip
> As you read "Ana's Project," think about Ana's goals, what she does to reach her goals, and how she changes as a result of her experiences.

Ana's Project

"Hurry up, Ana!" her brother, Pablo, yelled from the soccer field. "The game is starting!"

Ana grabbed her shoes and socks from the car and slammed the door. A boy she knew from school stood beside the car, watching.

"Are you playing soccer today?" Justin asked.

"Sure!" Ana said. "Aren't you?"

"No, I can't," was all that he said. Then he walked away, looking sadly at the soccer field.

Later that night, Ana asked her parents about Justin. "Why doesn't he play soccer with us?" she asked.

"Not everybody can afford it," her mother replied. "We had to pay a fee for you to play."

"Why can't he afford it?" Ana asked.

"I don't know. Maybe his parents don't have the extra money."

"It doesn't seem fair that both Pablo and I can play and Justin can't. Could we pay the fee for him?" Ana asked.

"Your mother and I can't afford that," her father replied. "According to your coach, there are ten kids who want to play soccer, but their parents can't afford to pay the fee. I'm afraid that there's nothing we can do to help them."

Ana couldn't stop thinking about Justin. Even though her parents couldn't do anything to help him, maybe she could find a way!

The next day, Ana contacted Mrs. Eisen, the president of the Parent-Teacher Association of her school, and told her about Justin's problem.

"We don't have extra money for that," Mrs. Eisen said. "Yet maybe I can help you kids do something—that is, if you want to work."

The next week, Ana and Mrs. Eisen thought of a strategy, or plan, to solve the problem. Ana organized all the students in her class to sponsor a bake sale. They spent several days baking pies, cakes, cookies, and brownies. On Saturday morning, they set up a table at the mall in their community. Many shoppers stopped to buy the baked goods. By the end of the afternoon, they had earned $450.

In the meantime, Ana and Mrs. Eisen spoke with the owner of Parton's Electronics. Mr. Parton donated, or contributed, a 31-inch television set. Ana's soccer team then sold raffle tickets for the television set. At the end of the second week, the team had earned another $600.

A few weeks later, Ana's soccer team was playing a game. Her mother had come to watch. Justin waved to them before he joined the other players on the field. "I'm so glad Justin is playing today," Ana's mother said. "Are you feeling good about what you did for him and the other kids?"

"Well, sort of," Ana said. Then she paused. "No, not really. I think I should do more to help people."

Ana had no idea what she wanted to do or how she should do it. Then late in the summer, she read a newspaper story about floods that had destroyed homes in nine states along the Mississippi River. She realized that children probably lived in many of those homes. They had probably lost all their clothes and toys. Ana imagined how sad they must be feeling. "There must be a way to help them," she thought.

Ana asked her soccer team to help her begin a clothing drive, or group effort, for the flood victims. Soon people were bringing boxes filled with clothes to Ana's garage. People who didn't have clothes to bring donated money. Ana used this money to pay for shipping costs. In a few weeks, everyone in town found out about Ana's project. Even the local news broadcast a story about the work that Ana and her soccer team were doing.

"You're doing a great thing," Ana's mother said to her after the last box was sent to the Red Cross in Arkansas. Ana just shook her head.

"What's wrong, Ana?" her father asked.

"It's not enough!" Ana cried. "There are thousands of people who are homeless. They need clothes and food. They'll need millions of dollars to rebuild their homes."

"Ana, you can't help everybody," her mother said. Ana was not convinced.

Later that night, Ana's father was working at his computer. He told Ana that he was online, or connected to other computer users on the Internet.

"Whom can you talk to on the Internet?" Ana asked.

"Just about anybody," her father said. "Anybody who is connected to the Internet, that is."

Then Ana had an idea. It was a big idea.

"About how many people would that be?" she asked her father. "Thousands?"

"More."

"A million?"

"Oh, yes, easily," her father said. "I'm sure it would be millions. The Internet connects people all over the world."

"Could I talk to big companies—companies that could make donations?" Ana asked.

"Sure," her father replied. "You could leave messages on their home pages."

"Then I've got a plan!" Ana shouted. "I'll need your help."

The next week, Ana and her father were very busy. First, he helped her set up a nonprofit organization, a company that does not make a profit. They named their company Project Flood. Ana and the soccer team asked their coach, the school principal, Mrs. Eisen, and Ana's parents to be on the company's board of directors, or group of advisors.

With Ana's father's help, Project Flood went online. On the Internet, Ana explained the problem. She then described what Project Flood was trying to do. She asked for clothing for the flood victims. She contacted children's clothing companies and asked for clothes of all sizes. She contacted shoe companies and asked for free shoes.

Every day after school, Ana and the soccer team opened boxes of clothing and letters containing checks. They sorted the clothing according to size and deposited the money in a special checking account. Clothes had been sent from all over the United States and Canada. A large box even came from a family in London, England. Soon there was enough money for clothes and toys for thousands of children.

Ana and the soccer team went to a toy store, filled ten shopping carts with toys, and bought them all. Then they packed and sent them to the flood victims in the nine states.

After helping the flood victims, Ana did not stop. She heard about children who had traveled on a boat from Haiti to the United States and needed food and clothing. Project Flood collected food and clothing to help the Haitian children.

Every day, Ana read the newspaper and listened to the news. She wanted to help everyone she could. She was always looking for people her group could help.

One afternoon, Ana and several students were wrapping boxes of clothes for Project Flood. Justin walked into the garage. He watched for a few minutes. Then he came over to Ana. "I'd like to help, too," he said.

COMPREHENSION

1. What are the settings in this story?

_____

_____

_____

2. What are the two things that Ana did to help Justin and the other students who could not play soccer?

_____

_____

_____

3. What is Project Flood?

_____

_____

_____

4. How did Ana's father help her?

_____

_____

_____

5. What effect did Ana's fund-raising have on the flood victims?

_____

_____

_____

6. Draw a line to match each word to its correct meaning.

drive   **a.** contributed

donated   **b.** group effort

online   **c.** connected to other computer users

CRITICAL THINKING

1. Do you think that Ana feels differently about helping others at the end of the story than she did at the beginning? Explain.

   _____

   _____

2. Describe how you think Ana's parents feel about their daughter's efforts.

   _____

3. Describe what you think is the theme, or message, of this story.

   _____

4. Explain why Justin wants to help Ana's group.

   _____

5. State why you think so many people give clothes and money to Project Flood.

   _____

SKILL FOCUS: CHARACTER

1. Who is the main character in the story?

   _____

2. What problem first concerns Ana?

   _____

   _____

3. What goal does Ana set to solve this problem?

   _____

   _____

4. Describe how Ana reaches her first goal.

   _____

   _____

5. What is Ana's second goal?

   _____

   _____

6. Describe how Ana reaches her second goal.

   _____

   _____

   _____

7. How does Ana change as a result of her experiences?

   _____

   _____

Reading-Writing Connection

What organizations in your community help people in need? On a separate sheet of paper, write a paragraph persuading people to contribute to one of these organizations.

Skill: Fact and Opinion

BACKGROUND INFORMATION

In "Hiking the Inca Trail," a teenager named Kristen describes in her diary the hike her family took on the ancient Inca Trail in South America. Between the 1200s and the 1500s, the Inca civilization grew in the Andes Mountains. Every year, many Incas traveled along the Inca Trail to visit the royal city of Machu Picchu. After Spanish invaders defeated the Incas in the 1500s, Machu Picchu was forgotten for centuries. Then, in 1911, an American explorer rediscovered the city in the jungles of Peru.

SKILL FOCUS: Fact and Opinion

Social studies articles usually include statements of fact and statements of opinion. A **fact** is a statement that can be checked or proven. Read the following fact.

The Incas lived in what is now Peru, Bolivia, and Chile in South America.

Readers can check this fact in reference books. They can also travel to South America and see the ruins of Inca civilization for themselves.

An **opinion** is a statement that cannot be proven or checked. It is someone's judgment or feelings about a subject. Words that show values and feelings often signal an opinion. Words such as *should, good, like, believe, important,* and *best* often occur in opinions. Read the following opinion.

The Incas were the best builders of their time.

The statement above makes a judgment. You could try to find facts that support the opinion, but you could not prove it true or false.

▶ Fill in the Fact and Opinion Chart in the next column with these statements.

The view from Machu Picchu is one of the most beautiful in South America.

Every year, thousands of tourists visit the ruins of Machu Picchu.

Fact	Opinion

CONTEXT CLUES: Details

Some context clues are **details**. In the sentences below, look for details that explain the meaning of the underlined word.

Anthropology is a science that studies human beings. An __anthropologist__ will sometimes travel great distances to study a culture firsthand. The scientist focuses on the culture's customs, origins, and development.

Details in all three sentences help explain the meaning of the word *anthropologist*—a scientist who studies human beings, travels far to study cultures, and is interested in the customs, origins, and development of people.

▶ Circle the details in the following sentence that help you figure out what *exhaustion* means.

It's so beautiful. I'm glad we're all ready to drop from __exhaustion__ and can't walk any farther.

In the next selection, use detail context clues to help you figure out the meanings of the underlined words *altitude, condors,* and *descent.*

┌─ **Strategy Tip** ─┐

As you read "Hiking the Inca Trail," be sure to distinguish the author's statements of fact from the author's opinions. Use the facts in the selection to help you draw conclusions about the Inca civilization.

HIKING THE INCA TRAIL

AUGUST 6, DAY 1: So much has happened in the past few days. On Sunday, we took an airplane to Lima, the capital of Peru. Monday, we drove to Cuzco (kOOS Ko) and walked around the city. It was difficult to walk uphill. Dad said that was because Cuzco is about 11,000 feet above sea level, and we needed to get used to the altitude. Even Victor was panting!

I've hiked a lot with my family, but we've never hiked in the Andes Mountains. This trip was Mom's idea, because she's an **anthropologist** (an thrə PAHL ə jist). Anthropology is a science that studies human beings. An anthropologist will sometimes travel great distances to study a culture firsthand. The scientist focuses on the culture's customs, origins, and development. Mom said this trip will be an education—a trip we'll never forget.

Today we started hiking a little past the village of Ollantaytambo (OH yan tay TAM boh). We followed the Urubamba River for a few miles and watched a red and yellow train passing below us.

It's winter in South America. Although it's the dry season, it's really warm today. Dad said that's because Peru is so near the equator. The sun is really strong, so we have to wear sunglasses and put on plenty of sunscreen.

We walked past small villages, and I bought a soft drink. As I walked, I looked at my dirty shorts and felt a blister starting on my left heel. However, I didn't stop for long, because Victor was way ahead. I didn't want him to think I couldn't keep up.

After hiking for about seven miles, we camped beside a stream and had dinner. As I write, I am wondering what my friend Dawn is doing tonight. She's probably going to the movies with Sophia. Suddenly I feel very homesick.

August 7, Day 2: What a surprise this morning! We woke up, broke camp, hiked for about a mile, and came to the Temple of the Hummingbird, which is an ancient Inca ruin. Victor and I explored the temple and found a place where Mom says they used to tie up condors. The Incas used these giant birds to send and receive messages across long distances, just as people today used falcons and pigeons. Mom also said that when the Incas began their journey to Machu Picchu, they had to pass through the Temple of the Hummingbird before they could begin their **pilgrimage** (PIL grə mij).

The rest of the day was awful. We had to hike and hike, all uphill. Victor walked ahead, as usual, trying to show me how strong he is. Big brothers! They always show off!

I'm still not used to the altitude, so I took about 20 steps and had to rest for a few seconds. Sometimes my heart felt as though it was going to explode. I think that I have two blisters now.

When we reached the second campsite, I helped Victor put up the tent, but I was exhausted. Dad had a headache and felt weak, so he went to bed right after supper. Mom said he has altitude sickness.

We are camping on a mountainside that looks straight at the snow-covered peaks of Mount Veronica. It's so beautiful. I'm glad we're all ready to drop from exhaustion and can't walk any farther. It's cold tonight, and I had to put on my sweater and down vest. I feel lucky to be here in the Andes Mountains, overlooking Mount Veronica. The Incas were very wise to spend so much time walking on this beautiful trail.

August 8, Day 3: Today we climbed and climbed and finally reached the Pass of the Eternal Woman. It's the first pass on the Inca Trail, and it is almost 14,000 feet high. That's almost three miles above sea level! By the time we reached the top of the pass, there were about 30 people waiting for us. I met a boy named Mario. He is my age, and he lives in Lima, but he doesn't know much English. I don't know much Spanish, so it was difficult to talk to him.

✔ I made an important decision today. I'm going to study Spanish next year, and I'm going to be serious about it this time! Learning new languages is very important when you travel. There was so much I wanted to talk to Mario about. All I could say was, *Cómo se llama*? He answered my question and said, "Mario." That's how I know his name.

After crossing the pass, we started hiking downhill through the Valley of the Rainbows. Just before lunch, we reached a place called Runkuracay (ROON kur rah KAY). The trail had turned into thousands of stone steps that the Incas had built here hundreds of years ago. From here on, the Royal Road was clearly defined. We looked back and saw the valley that we had walked through and the Pass of the Eternal Woman.

We climbed over the second pass, and I started to get hungry. However, Mom said that we had to wait until we reached the ruin called Sayacmarca (SAY yah MARK ah). I asked why there were so many ruins on the trail to Machu Picchu. Mom said that the Incas needed somewhere to stay at night along the way, so the buildings were placed exactly one day's walk from one another.

When we finally reached the circular structure, I groaned when I saw how high it was on the mountainside. My legs screamed for mercy as I climbed the hundred steps up the side. My legs forgave me after we feasted on slices of cantaloupe and peanut butter and jelly sandwiches.

After lunch, we began to walk through dense jungle. The trail is pretty flat and made of smooth stones that are built into the hillside. I knew that if I took one false step, I would fall into the jungle below and never be heard from again. I walked very carefully. I almost forgot! We passed through a very dark cave that was made naturally by two large rocks. Victor and I stopped and leaned against the side and felt the cold earth against our backs. For just a moment, I felt glad to have him as a brother—and I don't get those feelings often!

It's funny. With every step I took today, I felt stronger and stronger. We must have hiked more than 12 or 13 miles before we stopped at the last pass to camp. As I looked at the mountains, I forgot that tomorrow we will reach Machu Picchu.

August 9, Day 4: The <u>descent</u> from the pass is really quite steep, but the Incas constructed a series of steps that helped us. Within minutes, we stood at the site of the Temple in the Clouds and looked at the valley below. Mom said that we were at 12,000 feet, but we will descend about 4,000 feet to Machu Picchu.

We stopped for lunch at Wiñay Wayna, another temple built on the side of a mountain. Looking down, we could see the Urubamba River far away, probably a mile below us. Behind the temple, there are two fountains, where we washed our hands and face. The Incas believed that if you bathed in this water, you could heal parts of yourself that were sick and stay young forever. That's why this temple has the English name of the Temple of Eternal Youth.

After lunch, we began our final descent. The slope was more gentle, and we moved at a pretty rapid pace, eager to find the royal city below. We traveled through more dense jungle. We passed purple orchids, and I picked up a thick, pulpy white flower on the ground. I looked up, trying to find the tree from which it had fallen. It was so tall, I couldn't find it. I began to walk more slowly to enjoy the walk. I don't know when I might make this walk again.

We reached the entrance of Machu Picchu by midafternoon. The door of the city is open now. Yet long ago, only the Incas could pass through and

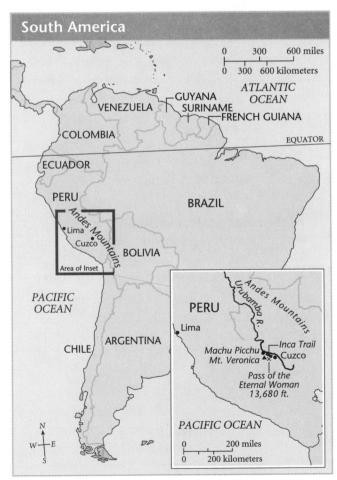

The Inca Trail was used to travel to the royal city of Machu Picchu.

LESSON 21 Fact and Opinion **69**

enter the city. We walked quietly through the entrance and thought about how the city must have looked more than 500 years ago, long before it was abandoned.

This vision of the ancient world is well worth the struggle we had to reach it. We walked through the quarry, where the stones were cut for the buildings and sculptures. Mom showed us the temple, where the priests performed ceremonies. She pointed out how the buildings were made to lean inward, to protect them from earthquakes. She led us to the place where the people once lived. We could still see the terraces where the farmers had grown food and crops.

Most of the structures still proudly stand in the Royal City. Llamas graze on the grass, and tourists walk the streets and explore the temples and tombs.

I thought that a few hundred years ago, a teenaged girl just like me had probably lived here. What did she do all day? What clothes did she wear? What was important to her? Who were her friends? What was her family like? Did she go to school?

There is so much about the Incas I don't know, so much I don't understand. Understanding the past is the best way to enrich your life. I remind myself that there is tomorrow. I have plenty of time to learn more!

COMPREHENSION

1. In what country did Kristen and her family hike?

   _____

2. Why did the family decide to go hiking there?

   _____

3. Based on the selection and the map on page 69, match each place in column A with its description in column B.

A	B
_____ Bolivia, Chile, Ecuador, Colombia, and Brazil	**a.** the mountains of Peru
_____ Andes	**b.** the countries that surround Peru
_____ Lima	**c.** the capital of Peru
_____ Pacific Ocean	**d.** the water that borders Peru on the west

4. **a.** Based on the inset map of the Inca Trail, exactly how high was the first pass? _____

   b. What river passes below Machu Picchu and through Cuzco? _____

5. Complete each sentence with the correct word below.

   altitude   condors   descent

   a. The _____ from the mountaintop was gradual and well marked.

   b. If you are at sea level in a coastal city, you are at a very low _____.

   c. _____ are very large birds used by the Incas to carry messages over long distances.

1. Describe how Kristen changed from the first day to the fourth day of the hike.

   _____

   _____

   _____

   _____

2. Circle the letter of the sentence below that tells the main idea of the paragraph with a ✓ next to it.

   a. Kristen wishes more people spoke English.

   b. Mario doesn't understand Spanish.

   c. Kristen wants to study Spanish so that she can speak to Spanish-speaking people.

   d. Kristen wants to travel all over the world and talk to people in their languages.

3. Conclude how Kristen's visit to Machu Picchu affected her.

   _____

   _____

   _____

4. How would you describe the Incas? On the lines, list three facts from Kristen's diary that support your conclusions.

   _____

   _____

   _____

   _____

   _____

   _____

SKILL FOCUS: FACT AND OPINION

Identify each of the following statements as a fact or an opinion by writing *F* or *O* on the line. For each opinion, underline the word or words that signal that the statement is based on the writer's feeling, judgment, or value.

_____ 1. Cuzco is about 11,000 feet above sea level.

_____ 2. Learning new languages is very important when you travel.

_____ 3. The Incas were very wise to spend so much time walking on this beautiful trail.

_____ 4. Understanding the past is the best way to enrich your life.

_____ 5. The Temple of Hummingbird is an ancient Inca ruin.

_____ 6. Peru is near the equator.

_____ 7. The Pass of the Eternal Woman is the first pass on the Inca Trail.

_____ 8. This vision of the ancient world is well worth the struggle we had to reach it.

Reading-Writing Connection

Picture yourself hiking the Inca Trail. Which part would interest you most? On a separate sheet of paper, write a diary entry describing what you see and telling why it interests you.

LESSON 22

Skill: Cause and Effect

BACKGROUND INFORMATION

"The Alien Invaders," is about the effects that alien plants and animals can have in a new environment. Some plants and animals are native to an environment. Others have been introduced from distant places. These nonnative plants and animals are called "exotics" or "aliens." Many alien species are harmless. Others cause serious damage to native species.

SKILL FOCUS: Cause and Effect

A **cause** is an event that makes something happen. An **effect** is what happens as a result of a cause. In a cause-and-effect relationship, one event causes another event to occur. To find an effect, ask, "What happened?" To find a cause, ask, "Why did it happen?" The words *because, since, due to,* and *as a result* often signal cause-and-effect relationships.

Sometimes two or more causes produce a single effect, as in the paragraph below.

The six muskrats found plenty of food in their new home. There were no natural predators, or enemies, to bother them. The earth dikes of the Netherlands, which kept out the sea, made a fine habitat for the animals. As a result, millions of muskrats were soon tunneling through the dikes.

You can show the multiple causes and their single effect in a graphic organizer like the following.

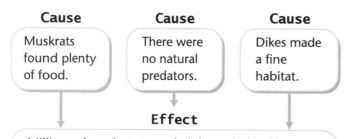

Cause	Cause	Cause
Muskrats found plenty of food.	There were no natural predators.	Dikes made a fine habitat.

Effect

Millions of muskrats tunneled through the dikes.

▶ Read the following sentences. Then fill in the Cause-and-Effect Chart in the next column.

Over time, the muskrats weakened the dikes. The sea threatened to break through and flood the countryside. The Dutch had to repair and rebuild the dikes at great cost.

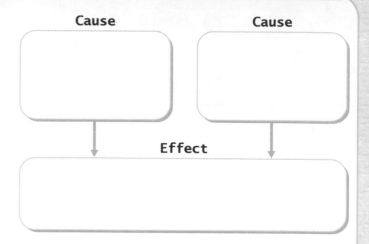

Cause	Cause

Effect

CONTEXT CLUES: Appositive Phrases

Some context clues are **appositive phrases**. An appositive phrase explains the meaning of a word that comes right before it. The phrase is usually set off from the word by commas and often by the word *or*.

Read the sentence below. What appositive phrase explains the meaning of the underlined word?

*Some nonnative species have been **eradicated**, or wiped out, in this country.*

If you don't know the meaning of *eradicated*, the appositive phrase *or wiped out* can help you.

▶ Circle the appositive phrase that explains the meaning of the underlined word in the following sentence.

*Animals and plants have always **migrated**, or moved from place to place.*

As you read the following selection, use appositive phrases to find the meanings of the underlined words *repel, quarantined,* and *nocturnal.*

> **Strategy Tip**
>
> As you read "The Alien Invaders," think about each alien species described. What effect did each one have on its new environment? What were the causes of each effect?

The Alien Invaders

ONE HUNDRED YEARS AGO, there were no muskrats in the Netherlands. Then in 1906, Dutch fur traders released six muskrats that they had brought from the United States. The fur traders hoped the muskrats would multiply so they could trap the mammals for their fur.

The fur traders were not disappointed. The six muskrats found plenty of food in their new home. There were no natural predators (PRED ə tərz), or enemies, to bother them. The earth dikes of the Netherlands, which kept out the sea, made a fine **habitat** (HAB ə tat) for the animals. As a result, millions of muskrats were soon tunneling through the dikes.

Over time, the muskrats weakened the dikes. The sea threatened to break through and flood the countryside. The Dutch had to repair and rebuild the dikes at great cost. They also hired hundreds of trappers to catch muskrats. Even so, no permanent solution to the Dutch muskrat problem has been found yet.

The story of the muskrats is not unique. All over the world, nonnative, or **alien** (AY lee ən), plants and animals are moving into new habitats.

Species on the Move

Animals and plants have always migrated, or moved from place to place. Seeds float on the wind and are carried by birds and animals. In the past, animals have crossed temporary ice bridges. They have even drifted on ocean currents, clinging to driftwood. Few species, however, moved very far or very often in these ways.

During the last few centuries, advances in transportation and worldwide trade have helped plants and animals move around the world. It is not uncommon, for example, for snakes to crawl into the wheel wells of airplanes and hop from country to country. Insects inside fruit or wood are shipped around the world. Sailors load water into the hulls of their ships to keep the ships stable. As a result, they carry tiny water creatures from continent to continent.

Some animals, like the Dutch muskrats, are deliberately introduced into new habitats. Other introductions are accidental. Nonnative pet birds and snakes, for example, may escape from cages and establish themselves in the wild. Either way, the effects can be dramatic.

Import From Australia

Over thousands of years, certain plants and animals have learned to share the same space. They make connections that allow them all to survive. This type of **ecosystem** (EE koh SIS təm) ticks along like a smoothly running clock.

For thousands of years, the Florida Everglades was such an ecosystem. Countless insects lived in the many plants and trees. The insects provided food for birds and reptiles. Larger animals then ate the birds and reptiles.

In 1936, melaleuca (MEL ə LOO kə) trees were imported from Australia. Florida lumberjacks hoped the new trees would produce inexpensive lumber in the supposedly "useless" Everglades wetlands. Today melaleuca trees have taken over 500,000 acres of the Everglades. They crowd out native plants and drain water from the swamps.

To make matters worse, the Australian trees repel, or drive away, Florida insects. So melaleuca forests provide no food or habitats for insect-eating birds and reptiles. The invasion of the melaleucas has threatened or destroyed various living things, disrupting the ecosystem in the Everglades environment.

Good Effects and Bad Effects

Not all imported species are dangerous. In fact, 98 percent of the American food supply comes from plants and animals that are not native to North America. Wheat, rice, and oats, for example, were brought here by early settlers. Beef and chicken are imports, too. So are many of our favorite fruits and vegetables.

Other alien species are cause for serious concern. These species threaten our environment and damage our economy. In the year 2000, Americans spent about $123 billion fighting dangerous alien species. Let's look at three of these alien species and the problems they cause.

Three Alien Pests

Alien weeds cost the nation's economy about $35.5 billion a year. One of the worst weeds is kudzu (KUD zoo). At the 1876 Philadelphia Exhibition, Japan had an exhibit featuring this exotic plant. Kudzu attracted many admirers. Visitors to this World's Fair took cuttings of the plant to grow at home.

Kudzu grew best in the South. People there planted it for several reasons. The vine was attractive, with purple flowers and the scent of grapes. Cattle and other livestock ate the fast-growing plant. Kudzu also restored nitrogen to worn-out soil. The government was so impressed that it paid people to plant kudzu.

Today kudzu is a serious problem in the South. Kudzu vines grow tall around telephone poles and ruin the electrical transformers at the top the poles. Kudzu covers road signs and causes accidents. Able to smother 100-foot-tall trees, kudzu has killed off entire forests. Power companies, railroad workers, and traffic departments spray, burn, and cut kudzu. So far, it has been a losing battle.

Zebra mussels are causing serious problems in our waterways. The nickel-sized shellfish were first sighted in our country in Lake Erie in 1988. They probably traveled there by ship from Europe.

Zebra mussels multiply rapidly. A single mussel can have 50 million offspring! By 1999, the zebra mussels had spread to 12 states.

Zebra mussels are making life difficult along the nation's waterways. Growing in thick mats, they clog water pipes, boat engines, and other equipment. The messy invaders coat boats and docks. They smother native shellfish. By eating all the available food, the mussels crowd out desirable fish.

Starlings are shiny black birds with starlike white spots. The first starlings were brought to New York City from Europe in 1890. These black birds adapted quickly in the United States. Spreading from coast to coast, they numbered over 200 million by 1960. During those same years, the population of native songbirds declined.

Why were the starlings thriving? For one thing, starlings have better vision than most birds and can find food faster. Starlings are also strong enough to push other birds from their own nests. By taking over much of the available food in many habitats, starlings have made it difficult for other birds to survive.

Zebra mussels multiply rapidly. They crowd out native fish and shellfish and destroy equipment on our nation's waterways.

Traveling in huge flocks, starlings cause other problems, too. They can destroy an entire fruit crop in a few hours. Starling flocks have also flown into airplane engines with disastrous results. The flocks also kill trees and damage parks with their droppings.

What Should Be Done?

How can people and governments stop the spread of destructive alien species? Nowadays governments check imported food for alien species. Pets and other animals from overseas are

Huge flocks of starlings crowd out other birds, destroy fruit crops, and kill trees.

quarantined (KWOR ən teend), or kept separate, for a period time to make sure they are safe. People can no longer introduce new species just because they think it is a good idea.

Some nonnative species have been eradicated, or wiped out, in this country. During the 1920s, for example, Eurasian water chestnuts were grown in the pools on the mall in Washington, D.C. Somehow the species spread to the Potomac River and other waterways. Over 10,000 acres of water were soon choking under the plants. Luckily, swift action removed them before the situation got out of control.

In the mid-1990s, Asian long-horned beetles arrived here in packing crates from China. They quickly began to infest shade trees in New York City and Chicago. City officials cut down and burned all the trees in some blocks to eradicate the beetles.

Using other species to control unwanted aliens is another solution. In California, for example, an insect called the cotton scale threatened to destroy the state's crop of oranges. Growers brought in a type of beetle from Australia, a natural predator of the scale. The crop was saved.

Controlling one new species with another new species has its dangers, though. In Hawaii, rats arrived in the 1870s and became a big problem. Farmers imported mongooses from India to fight the rats. The rats, however, were nocturnal, or active during the night. The mongooses hunted by day. Since the mongooses rarely saw the rats, they feasted on native birds instead. As a result, several types of birds almost became extinct.

All living things are connected in a delicate web of life. It is up to all of us to protect the balance of nature around us. Alien species remind us how easily this balance can be upset.

COMPREHENSION

1. Why were muskrats introduced to the Netherlands in 1906?

   _____

   _____

   _____

2. What are some nonnative species that make up a major part of our food supply?

   _____

   _____

   _____

3. Find the paragraph with a ✔ next to it. Underline the sentence that tells its main idea.

4. Why did people in the South plant kudzu?

   _____

   _____

   _____

5. What unexpected effect did mongooses have on native animals in Hawaii?

   _____

   _____

   _____

6. Write the meaning of each word.

   repel   _____

   quarantined   _____

   nocturnal   _____

1. Explain why the environment of the Everglades would be better if insects attacked the melaleuca trees there.

    _____

    _____

2. Explain why is it often very difficult to eradicate a destructive alien plant or animal.

    _____

    _____

3. Tell how scientists might use a new species to fight kudzu.

    _____

    _____

SKILL FOCUS: CAUSE AND EFFECT

On the lines, write three causes for each effect. You may look back at the selection.

1. **Effect:** Today kudzu is a serious problem in the South.

    a. **Cause:** _____

    b. **Cause:** _____

    c. **Cause:** _____

2. **Effect:** Zebra mussels are making life difficult along the nation's waterways.

    a. **Cause:** _____

    b. **Cause:** _____

    c. **Cause:** _____

3. **Effect:** Starlings thrive while native songbirds decline.

    a. **Cause:** _____

    b. **Cause:** _____

    c. **Cause:** _____

Reading-Writing Connection

Use a library or the Internet to find out more about the problems caused by a nonnative species in the United States. On a separate sheet of paper, create a cause-and-effect chart to show how this species is affecting our environment. Then use the chart to write a short report on the subject.

Skill: Word Problems

BACKGROUND INFORMATION

In "Solving Word Problems," you will learn five steps to help you solve word problems. Being able to solve word problems will often help you in daily life. For example, suppose you go to the mall with a $20 bill. You want to buy a CD that costs $11.69 and a shirt on sale for $6.79. Will you have enough money for both? The only way to know for sure is by solving a real-life word problem.

SKILL FOCUS: Word Problems

The following five steps will help you solve word problems.

1. **Read the problem.** Be sure that you know all the words, especially the labels that are used with each number. Think about what the problem is asking you to do. In your mind, picture the information you are given. If necessary, reread the problem to make sure you understand it.

2. **Decide how to find the answer.** Drawing a picture of the information in the problem may be helpful. Decide whether you should add, subtract, multiply, or divide. Look for key words in the last sentence to help you figure out which operation to use. Then write the mathematical sentence that will solve the problem.

3. **Estimate the answer.** Round the numbers in the problem so that you can quickly figure out "about" how much the answer should be. This is called *estimating* or *making an estimate*.

4. **Carry out the plan.** Solve the mathematical sentence that you wrote in Step 2. Do the arithmetic that will give you the answer.

5. **Reread the problem.** Does the answer make sense? How close is it to your estimate? If your answer is not close to the estimate, start over again at Step 1.

▶ Go back to the word problem described in the Background Information on this page. If you have a $20 bill, can you buy a CD that costs $11.69 and a shirt that costs $6.79?

Write the math sentence that will solve the problem. _____

Now estimate the answer. _____

WORD CLUES

Some words in math problems are clues that suggest whether you should add or subtract. The words *together* and *sum*, for example, are signals to add. The phrases *how many more* and *how much greater* are signals to subtract. Some other words that signal subtraction are *difference, more, less, shorter, longer,* and *left*. These signal words are usually in the last sentence of a word problem.

▶ Circle the word in the last sentence of the following problem that is a signal that you need to subtract.

Jay went to the mall with $20 and spent $12.50 on a CD. How much money did he have left ?

Strategy Tip

In "Solving Word Problems," you will learn how to use the five steps to solve word problems about people living in cities and states. Be sure to work through each step carefully.

Solving Word Problems

Every ten years, the U.S. Census collects facts about the populations of American states and cities. Suppose the following facts are known.

In 2000, New York had a population of 18.9 million. In 2000, Georgia had 8.2 million people.

These facts can be put together to answer this question. *How many more people lived in New York than in Georgia in 2000?*

Read the Problem

New York had a population of 18.9 million. Georgia had a population of 8.2 million. How many more people lived in New York than in Georgia?

Be sure that you know the label that is used with each number fact. Are there any words that you do not know? If so, look them up in a dictionary to find their meanings. What question does the problem ask? Often the question is asked in the last sentence. *How many more people lived in New York than in Georgia in 2000?* Read the problem again.

Decide How to Find the Answer

You need to decide how to put the facts together to answer the question. Facts can be put together in the following four ways.

- Add to combine groups.
- Subtract to compare groups.
- Multiply to combine many small groups of the same size.
- Divide to break down one big group into smaller groups.

Which way should you put the facts together to answer the question? The word *more* is a key word that tells you to compare information. Because the question asks you to compare, you need to subtract.

Now you can write a mathematical sentence to help you answer the question.

You know two things: 18.9 million people lived in New York, and 8.2 million people lived in Georgia. This is your mathematical sentence.

$$18.9 - 8.2 = n$$

The letter n stands for the number you are trying to find.

Estimate the Answer

Round 18.9 million to 19 million. Round 8.2 million to 8 million. Subtract 8 million from 19 million.

$$19 - 8 = 11$$

Your estimate is 11 million people.

Carry Out the Plan

$$18.9 - 8.2 = 10.7 \text{ people}$$

Reread the Problem

New York had 10.7 million more people than Georgia. Does this answer make sense? How close is this answer to your estimate?

Use the five steps to solve the following problem.

Read: *In 2000, New York had a population of 18.9 million. The average household had 2.6 people. About how many households were there in New York?*

Decide: Use division to break down one big group into smaller groups. Write a mathematical sentence to answer the question.

$$18.9 \div 2.6 = n$$

Estimate: Round 18.9 million to 19 million. Round 2.6 to 3. Divide 19 million by 3.

$$19 \div 3 = 6.3$$

Your estimate is 6.3 million households.

Carry Out: $18.9 \div 2.6 = 7.3$ million households

Reread: *There were about 7.3 million households in New York in 2000.*

Fill in the blanks to complete the sentences below.

1. In a word problem, the question is usually

   asked in _____ sentence.

2. The label _____ is used in the first
   problem on page 78. In the second problem,

   the label _____ is used.

3. You _____ to combine groups,

   _____ to compare groups,

   _____ to combine many small

   groups of the same size, and _____
   to break down one big group into smaller
   groups.

CRITICAL THINKING

1. Which mathematical operation is similar to addition?

   _____

2. Which mathematical operation is similar to subtraction?

   _____

3. Identify the two mathematical operations that produce an answer that is greater than all
   the numbers in a problem.

   _____

4. Identify the two mathematical operations that produce an answer that is smaller than at
   least one of the numbers in a problem.

   _____

SKILL FOCUS: WORD PROBLEMS

Use the five steps to solve these problems. Write a mathematical sentence in the
Decide step.

1. **Read:** New Haven and Bridgeport are two Connecticut cities. They have areas of 48.9
   square kilometers and 41.4 square kilometers. What is the area of the two cities
   together?

   Decide: _____

   Estimate: _____

   Carry Out: _____

   Reread: _____

MATHEMATICS

2. **Read:** In 2000, there were about 3.3 million rental apartments in the state of New York. An average of 2.4 people lived in each apartment. About how many people rented apartments in New York?

Decide: _____

Estimate: _____

Carry Out: _____

Reread: _____

3. **Read:** In 1999, the average income per person in Pennsylvania was $28,676. The average income per person in Delaware was $30,685. How much greater was the income per person in Delaware?

Decide: _____

Estimate: _____

Carry Out: _____

Reread: _____

4. **Read:** In 1998, the population of Omaha, Nebraska, was about 371,291. The land area of Omaha was about 117 square miles. About how many people were there per square mile living in Omaha in 1998?

Decide: _____

Estimate: _____

Carry Out: _____

Reread: _____

5. **Read:** In 1998, Los Angeles had a population of 3,597,566. New York City had a population of 7,420,166. How many more people lived in New York City than in Los Angeles?

Decide: _____

Estimate: _____

Carry Out: _____

Reread: _____

Reading-Writing Connection

Find out the current population of your community. Then research the population of your community ten years ago. Use the information to write a word problem about how the population of your community has changed in the last ten years.

LESSON 24

Skill: Syllables

To help you pronounce a long word, divide the word into **syllables**. Then pronounce each syllable until you can say the whole word. There are several different ways of deciding how a word should be divided.

Compounds Words

A compound word is made up of two words. It must have at least two syllables. Always divide a compound word into syllables by separating it between the two smaller words first. If these smaller words have more than one syllable, it may be necessary to use another rule. However, you can pronounce most compound words if you first divide them into two smaller words.

A. Read each of the following compound words. Divide the word into two syllables by writing each of the two smaller words separately on the line next to the compound word. Then fill in the words necessary to complete the rule below.

1. homesick _____
2. raincoat _____
3. outline _____
4. steamship _____

5. snowfall _____
6. footprint _____
7. doorway _____
8. textbook _____

RULE: A compound word is divided into _____ between the _____ smaller words.

Words With Double Consonants

Use another rule for words with double consonants. Divide the word into two syllables between the two consonants. Then read each syllable.

B. Read each of the following double consonant words. Divide the word into syllables by writing each syllable separately on the line next to the word. Then fill in the words necessary to complete the rule below.

1. supper _____
2. happen _____
3. sudden _____
4. command _____

5. quarrel _____
6. suggest _____
7. cotton _____
8. sapphire _____

RULE: A word that has a _____ consonant is divided into syllables between the _____ consonants.

To help you pronounce a long word, divide the word into **syllables**. Then pronounce each syllable until you can say the whole word.

Words With a Prefix or Suffix

A prefix always has at least one sounded vowel. This means that a prefix always contains at least one syllable. You can divide a word that has a prefix between the prefix and the base word.

A. Divide each word below into two syllables between the prefix and the base word. Write each syllable separately on the line next to the word.

1. transport _____
2. return _____
3. precook _____
4. displace _____
5. refill _____
6. preview _____
7. distrust _____

8. untrue _____
9. distaste _____
10. inside _____
11. replant _____
12. disprove _____
13. undone _____
14. prepay _____

A suffix always has at least one sounded vowel. This means that a suffix always contains at least one syllable. You can divide a word that has a suffix between the base word and the suffix.

B. Divide each word below into two syllables between the base word and the suffix. Write each syllable separately on the line next to the word.

1. gladly _____
2. statement _____
3. teacher _____
4. helpful _____
5. frighten _____
6. breathless _____
7. shorten _____

8. pitcher _____
9. brightly _____
10. careful _____
11. beastly _____
12. broaden _____
13. creamy _____
14. handful _____

C. Fill in the word necessary to complete the following rule.

RULE: A word that has a prefix or _____ is divided into syllables between the prefix or suffix and the base word.

Skill: Syllables

To help you pronounce a long word, divide the word into **syllables**. Then pronounce each syllable until you can say the whole word.

Words With Two Consonants Between Two Sounded Vowels

Many words have two consonants between two sounded vowels. This rule will help you in dividing such words.

A. Say each word below listening to be sure that each syllable has only one vowel sound. Write each syllable separately on the line next to the word. Then fill in the words necessary to complete the rule below.

1. winter _____
2. order _____
3. picture _____
4. target _____
5. window _____
6. monkey _____

RULE: A word that has two _____ between two sounded _____ is divided into syllables between the two _____.

B. You can use this rule to divide words that you do not know how to pronounce. Divide each word below into two syllables by writing each syllable separately on the line next to the word.

1. husband _____
2. wonder _____
3. perhaps _____
4. garden _____
5. capture _____
6. Denver _____
7. convince _____
8. escape _____
9. expert _____
10. signal _____
11. enter _____
12. velvet _____
13. carbon _____
14. former _____
15. tender _____
16. admit _____
17. cactus _____
18. doctor _____
19. lantern _____
20. canvas _____
21. picnic _____
22. silver _____
23. napkin _____
24. helmet _____
25. circus _____
26. basket _____
27. shelter _____
28. number _____

Skill: Syllables

To help you pronounce a long word, divide the word into **syllables**. Then pronounce each syllable until you can say the whole word.

Words With One Consonant Between Two Sounded Vowels

Many words have only one consonant between two sounded vowels. The following rules will help you in dividing such words. The first rule will help you with words in which the first vowel is long. The second rule will help you with words in which the first vowel is short.

A. You can tell where to divide the words below into syllables by saying them. Say the word. Listen to be sure that each syllable has only one vowel sound. Write each syllable separately on the line next to the word. Then fill in the words necessary to complete the rule below.

1. music _____
2. climate _____
3. bacon _____

4. locate _____
5. notice _____
6. final _____

RULE: If a word has one _____ between two sounded _____,

with the first _____ long, the word is usually divided into syllables

before the _____.

B. You can use this rule to divide words into syllables. Divide each word below into two syllables by writing each syllable separately on the line next to the word.

1. later _____
2. nature _____
3. paper _____
4. hotel _____

5. fever _____
6. major _____
7. native _____
8. motor _____

Some words with a consonant between two sounded vowels do not follow the previous rule. They are divided after the consonant instead of before it. In these words, the first vowel is short instead of long.

C. Say each of the words below. Decide whether the first vowel is long or short. If it is short, divide the word into syllables after the consonant. Write each syllable separately on the line next to the word. Then fill in the words necessary to complete the rule on the next page.

1. rapid _____
2. travel _____
3. topic _____

4. wagon _____
5. petal _____
6. relish _____

RULE: If a word has one _____ between two sounded _____,

with the first vowel _____, the word is usually divided into syllables

after the _____.

D. You can use this rule to divide words into syllables. Divide each word below into syllables by writing each syllable separately on the line next to the word.

1. digit _____
2. magic _____
3. profit _____
4. seven _____
5. solid _____

6. medal _____
7. river _____
8. salad _____
9. visit _____
10. pedal _____

Words With Blends

The word *subtract* has three consonants between two sounded vowels. Because the blend *tr* stands for one sound, it is treated in the same way that a single consonant is treated. Divide the word between the consonant and the consonant blend: *sub tract.*

When you see a word that has three or more consonants between two vowels, find the blend and treat it as one consonant.

E. Circle the blend in each of the words below. Divide each word into two syllables by writing each syllable separately on the line next to the word.

1. children _____
2. congress _____
3. substance _____

4. purchase _____
5. hindrance _____
6. bolster _____

F. When a word ends in *-le*, the *-le* and the consonant before it make up a syllable, as in *cra dle* or *a ble*. Divide these words into syllables by writing each syllable on the line next to the word. Then fill in the words to complete the rule below.

1. bundle _____
2. jungle _____
3. gentle _____
4. bugle _____

5. tremble _____
6. candle _____
7. mantle _____
8. staple _____

RULE: Do not split a consonant _____ or a consonant and _____.

Treat a consonant blend or _____ and *-le* as if it were one consonant.

Skill: Understanding Word Origins

Roots, prefixes, and suffixes are word parts. You can often figure out the meaning of an unknown word if you know the meaning of each of its word parts. For example, the word *philosopher* comes from the Greek roots *philos,* which means "loving," and *sophos,* which means "wise." *Philosopher* means "someone who loves wisdom."

Latin Roots

Latin has been an important language since the days of the Roman Empire. During the Middle Ages, it became the language of scholars, or learned people, in Europe. By using Latin, scholars from different lands could easily communicate with one another. Most books from the Middle Ages were written in Latin, too. Today more than half of the words in the English language can be traced back to Latin.

Many of these words are related to law, government, and religion, such as *legislator* and *legislate. Legislator* means "one who makes the law," and *legislate* means "to make laws." Both are from the Latin root *leges,* which means "laws."

Greek Roots

Twenty-five hundred years ago, Greece was the center of learning for the entire Western world. Greece had the best government and the finest artists and writers. Once the Romans conquered Greece, they began to enjoy Greek art and writing so much that they made Greek words part of their own language. Some of these words are now part of the English language.

For example, the Greek word *kybernan,* which means "to steer or rule," became *gubernare* in Latin because it was easier for the Romans to pronounce. The English word *govern* comes from the Latin word.

More English words came from these Latin words of Greek origin. About 600 years ago, the people in Italy became more interested in learning than they had ever been before. They turned to the books, art, and language of Ancient Greece. Gradually more Greek words became part of the Latin language. Soon scholars all over the Western world were using Greek words that they had changed to fit into their own language.

For example, the word *telescope* is formed by combining the root *tele* and the root *scope.* If you know that *tele* means "far away" and *scope* means an "instrument for observing," you can figure out that *telescope* means "an instrument for observing things far away."

Knowing the meaning of *scope* helps you with the meaning of such words as *stethoscope, microscope,* and *kaleidoscope.* Knowing the meaning of *tele* helps you with the meaning of such words as *telegraph, television,* and *telephone.*

A. The word *port* comes from the Latin root *portare,* which means "to carry." Read each sentence below and underline the word with the root *port.*

1. Rowboats transport visitors from the mainland to the island.

2. Many American blue jeans are made for export to foreign countries.

3. José took the portable television set from the bedroom to the kitchen.

4. The porter put the suitcases into the trunk of the car.

5. We import much of our coffee from South American countries.

B. Write the underlined words from the sentences in Part A on the lines below. Then match each one with its meaning. Write the letter of the correct meaning on the line next to the word.

6. _____ ____   **a.** things that are carried out of

7. _____ ____   **b.** carry across

8. _____ ____   **c.** one who carries

9. _____ ____   **d.** able to be carried

10. _____ ____   **e.** carry into

C. Read the Latin and Greek word parts and their meanings. Then underline the Latin or Greek word part from the chart in each of the following words. Finally complete each sentence below by writing one of the eight words on the line.

Root	Meaning	Prefix	Meaning	Suffix	Meaning
aud (Latin)	to hear	*bi-* (Latin)	two	*-logy* (Greek)	study of
vis (Latin)	to see			*-phobia* (Greek)	fear of

1. audible   3. vision   5. claustrophobia   7. audition

2. biceps   4. zoology   6. bicycle   8. invisible

9. Some people are afraid of being in enclosed places. They have _____.

10. People who are interested in animals study animal life. This study is called _____.

11. To get a part in a play, an actor or actress performs at a hearing. There, his or her

    acting ability is tested. This is called an _____.

12. Some movies have ghosts you cannot see. You cannot see _____ ghosts.

D. Read the Greek word parts and their meanings. Then combine two of the word parts below to make a word that will complete each sentence. Write the word on the line.

Root	Meaning	Prefix	Meaning	Suffix	Meaning
scope	a device for seeing	*auto-*	self	*-cracy*	government
phone	sound	*demo-*	people		
graph	writing	*micro-*	very small		

1. A hair viewed under a _____ will appear larger than it really is.

2. The quiet man used a _____ so everybody in the room heard his speech.

3. The type of government in which one person rules is an _____.

4. The type of government of, for, and by the people is a _____.

Skill: Reading a Bus Schedule

If you have traveled by bus, you may have checked a **bus schedule.** A bus schedule lists the times the buses run and tells where the buses make stops. In most cities, the busiest time for buses is rush hour, when most people go to and come from work. More buses run during these hours because the need for the buses is much greater at that time.

This bus schedule shows where a bus on Route 44 stops. The times below each place show when a bus stops there. Read from left to right across each line to find out what time the bus going from Mount Vernon Place to North Shore Apartments makes each stop.

BUS ROUTE 44 — Northbound from Downtown

Monday through Friday

	MOUNT VERNON PLACE	RUXTON ROAD	GREEN-SPRINGS AVENUE	STEVENS VILLAGE MALL	PARK CREST ROAD	NORTH SHORE APARTMENTS
A.M.	7:30	7:45	7:49	7:52	7:55	7:59
	8:20	8:35	8:39	8:42	8:45	8:49
	9:30	9:45	9:49	9:52	9:55	9:59
	10:30	10:45	10:49	10:52	10:55	10:59
	11:30	11:45	11:49	11:52	11:55	11:59
P.M.	12:20	12:35	12:39	12:42	12:45	12:49
	2:10	2:25	2:29	2:32	—	2:39
	2:40	2:55	2:59	3:02	3:05	3:09
	3:10	3:25	3:29	3:32	—	3:39
	4:15	4:30	4:34	4:37	4:40	4:44
	4:40	5:01	5:05	5:08	5:11	5:15
	4:55	5:16	5:20	5:23	5:26	5:30
	5:05	5:26	5:30	5:33	5:36	5:40
	5:10	5:31	5:35	5:38	5:41	5:45
	5:15	5:36	5:40	5:43	5:46	5:50
	5:20	5:41	5:45	5:48	5:51	5:55
	5:30	5:51	5:55	5:58	6:01	6:05
	5:40	6:01	6:05	6:08	6:11	6:15
	5:50	6:11	6:15	6:18	6:21	6:25
	6:05	6:20	6:24	6:27	6:30	6:34
	6:30	6:45	6:49	6:52	6:55	6:59
	7:30	7:45	7:49	7:52	7:55	7:59
	8:30	8:45	8:49	8:52	8:55	8:59
	9:30	9:45	9:49	9:52	9:55	9:59

Saturday

	MOUNT VERNON PLACE	RUXTON ROAD	GREEN-SPRINGS AVENUE	STEVENS VILLAGE MALL	PARK CREST ROAD	NORTH SHORE APARTMENTS
A.M.	8:30	8:45	8:49	8:52	8:55	8:59
	11:30	11:45	11:49	11:52	11:55	11:59
P.M.	1:20	1:35	1:39	1:42	1:45	1:49
	2:40	2:55	2:59	3:02	3:05	3:09
	3:40	3:55	3:59	4:02	4:05	4:09
	4:15	4:30	4:34	4:37	4:40	4:44
	4:45	5:00	5:04	5:07	5:10	5:14
	5:15	5:30	5:34	5:37	5:40	5:44
	6:15	6:30	6:34	6:37	6:40	6:44
	7:15	7:30	7:34	7:37	7:40	7:44
	8:15	8:30	8:34	8:37	8:40	8:44
	9:15	9:30	9:34	9:37	9:40	9:44

Sunday and Holidays

	MOUNT VERNON PLACE	RUXTON ROAD	GREEN-SPRINGS AVENUE	STEVENS VILLAGE MALL	PARK CREST ROAD	NORTH SHORE APARTMENTS
A.M.	8:30	8:45	8:49	8:52	8:55	8:59
	11:30	11:45	11:49	11:52	11:55	11:59
P.M.	1:30	1:45	1:49	1:52	1:55	1:59
	3:30	3:45	3:49	3:52	3:55	3:59
	5:30	5:45	5:49	5:52	5:55	5:59

A. Use the information on the bus schedule to complete each sentence.

1. The name of the place where Bus Route 44 begins is _____.

2. The name of the place where Bus Route 44 ends is _____.

3. The first bus leaves Mount Vernon Place at _____ each weekday morning.

4. The last bus leaves Mount Vernon Place at _____ every Saturday evening.

5. It takes three minutes to go from Greensprings Avenue to _____.

6. The buses leaving Mount Vernon Place at 2:10 P.M. and 3:10 P.M. on weekdays do not make a stop at _____.

7. If you leave Mount Vernon Place by 4:15 P.M. any weekday, it takes 15 minutes to arrive at _____. However, if you leave at 5:50 P.M., it takes _____. It takes longer at this time probably because _____.

8. If you take the 3:55 P.M. bus on Saturday from Ruxton Road, you will arrive at _____ at 4:05 P.M.

B. Fill in the circle next to the answer to each question.

1. On Saturdays, when does the 8:15 P.M. bus from Mount Vernon Place arrive at Park Crest Road?

   ○ 8:44 P.M.   ○ 8:30 P.M.
   ○ 8:40 P.M.   ○ 8:42 P.M.

2. If you leave Ruxton Road on the 11:45 A.M. bus on a Sunday, what time will you arrive at North Shore Apartments?

   ○ 11:59 A.M.   ○ 11:49 P.M.
   ○ 11:59 P.M.   ○ 1:59 P.M.

3. What time does the last bus leave Mount Vernon Place on holidays?

   ○ 9:30 P.M.   ○ 5:45 P.M.
   ○ 9:44 P.M.   ○ 5:30 P.M.

4. On Saturdays, how many morning buses travel from Ruxton Road to the Stevens Village Mall?

   ○ two   ○ twelve
   ○ five   ○ seven

5. How many days a week does a 4:30 P.M. bus go from Ruxton Road to Stevens Village Mall?

   ○ five   ○ seven
   ○ six   ○ four

6. How many buses travel Route 44 between 4:00 P.M. and 6:00 P.M. on weekdays?

   ○ three   ○ eleven
   ○ ten   ○ nine

7. How long does it take to get from Mount Vernon Place to Greensprings Avenue on a Sunday?

   ○ 15 minutes   ○ 20 minutes
   ○ 21 minutes   ○ 19 minutes

8. To get to North Shore Apartments by 5:00 P.M. on Tuesday, when do you need to leave Stevens Village Mall?

   ○ 4:15 P.M.   ○ 5:08 P.M.
   ○ 4:37 P.M.   ○ 4:02 P.M.

Seeing Both Sides

LESSON 30

Skill: Point of View

BACKGROUND INFORMATION

In the selection "Rosa Parks," you will read the life story of one of the heroes of the American Civil Rights movement. During the 1950s, many African Americans began fighting against unjust laws in the South. These laws forced African American students to attend separate schools, apart from white students. They forced all African Americans to use separate public facilities, including drinking fountains, swimming pools, restrooms, and buses. In 1955, Rosa Parks refused to give up her seat on a bus to a white man. Her courage helped spark the Civil Rights Movement during the 1950s and 1960s.

SKILL FOCUS: Point of View

Every story has a narrator, or storyteller. The narrator tells the story from a certain **point of view**, or perspective. Some stories are told from the first-person point of view. Others are told from the third-person point of view.

In **first-person point of view**, a character in the story describes events from his or her own perspective. This character uses the pronouns *I, me, my,* and *we* to tell the story. An **autobiography** is one type of first-person writing. In an autobiography, a person tells the true story of his or her own life.

In **third-person point of view**, the storyteller, or narrator, is someone outside the story. This narrator uses the pronouns *he, she,* and *they* to tell what the characters think and do. A **biography** is one type of third-person writing. In a biography, an author tells the life story of another person.

▶ Read each part of a story in the next column. On the lines, write *first-person* or *third-person* to describe its point of view.

When he was 17, Harvey Gantt knew that the laws in the South were unfair. So he and his friends began sit-ins at "Whites Only" lunch counters.

_____

When I was 17, I asked my friends to join me in a sit-in so that we could change the unjust laws.

_____

CONTEXT CLUES: Details

The **details** in sentences are often context clues. Such details can help you figure out the meaning of a new word. In the sentences below, look for details that explain the meaning of the underlined word.

Parks had many skills that she had not been allowed to __employ__ in other jobs. She got to use them now.

If you are not sure what *employ* means, the details *many skills* and *got to use* can help you. To employ something is to use it.

▶ Read the following sentences. Circle details that help you figure out the meaning of *appeal*.

When someone loses a case in a local court, that person can __appeal,__ or ask another court to hear the case all over again. A higher court can then reverse, or change, the decision of the lower court.

In "Rosa Parks," look for details to help you figure out the meanings of the underlined words *segregated, league,* and *boycott.*

> ### Strategy Tip
>
> As you read the biography "Rosa Parks," think about the point of view the narrator includes.

ROSA PARKS

At 43, Rosa Parks sits at the front of a city bus after the Supreme Court ruling banned segregation on public buses and trains.

Rosa McCauley Parks was born in 1913. When she was a child, she lived on a farm near Tuskegee, Alabama, with her mother, grandparents, and brother.

Young Rosa McCauley often lay awake at night, listening for the sound of galloping horses. At that time, many African Americans lay awake in fear because a dangerous group of white men rode horses in the night. The men belonged to a group called the Ku Klux Klan. They dressed in white and wore hoods over their heads. They burned buildings and even killed people, but no one punished them for their crimes.

As Rosa McCauley grew up, she also learned that there were rules for African Americans. They could not drink from the same water fountains as white people. They could not eat at lunch counters in stores. African American children and white children could not go to the same schools. The schools for African American children were crowded and small, and some did not even have desks.

Schools were important to Rosa's family. Her mother had gone to college and had taught school. Rosa could read when she began school because her

mother had taught her. When Rosa was older, her mother returned to teaching, and Rosa was one of her students.

When Rosa was 11, her mother sent her to a new school, a private school for girls in Montgomery, Alabama. Her mother had saved money to pay for the school. Rosa studied such subjects as English and science, but she learned something even more important. Her mother taught her to believe in herself—and so did her new teachers.

When her school closed, Rosa went to Booker T. Washington Junior High. Later she took some high school courses, but when her mother became ill, Rosa had to drop out of school.

In time, Rosa met Raymond Parks, a barber. Rosa and Raymond got married. With her husband's help, Rosa Parks went back to school and received her high school diploma.

After high school, Parks took the jobs she could find. She worked in a hospital and did sewing at home, but there were not many job choices for African Americans back then. They also faced special problems on the job, and even getting to work could be a problem.

Most African Americans did not own cars, and the buses were <u>segregated</u> in Montgomery. African Americans could not sit in the front of the bus. They could sit only in the back. On a crowded bus, they had to give up their seats to white people. African Americans also had to pay their fare at the front of the bus. Then they had to get out of the bus, go to the door at the back, and get on again.

One day, Parks tried to break this rule. She got on at the front of the bus, paid her fare, and started down the aisle. The bus driver came toward her and grabbed her coat sleeve. He told her to get off the bus and use the back door to get back on. When she argued with him, he ordered her off the bus. She got off, and the bus left without her.

Rosa Parks believed in herself, and she was tired of being treated unfairly. She decided to do something about it. In 1943, Parks joined the

National Association for the Advancement of Colored People, or NAACP. The NAACP was a group of African Americans and white people working together to end segregation.

Parks had many skills that she had not been allowed to employ in other jobs. She got to use them now. She became secretary of the Alabama NAACP, and its president, Edgar Daniel Nixon, was very impressed with her work.

Parks and Nixon also worked together for the Montgomery Voters <u>League</u>. This group worked to make sure that all African Americans could vote. To vote in Alabama, African Americans had to pass a test on which they could not make a single mistake. Parks visited homes and helped people learn how to take the test.

Many white people tried to keep African Americans from voting. They warned Parks and Nixon that they would be in danger if they continued to help African Americans with the voting test. However, these threats did not stop Parks and Nixon.

Slowly the NAACP began making progress. The organization went to the United States Supreme Court to argue that segregated schools were unfair. In 1954, the Supreme Court agreed. The judges decided that separate schools did not provide equal education for African American children. This was a great victory. Rosa Parks did not stop working for justice then, though. She looked for more ways to end segregation.

Help came from Virginia Durr, a white woman for whom Parks worked. Durr convinced Parks to attend classes at the Highlander Folk School in Tennessee. People from all over the country went there to learn ways to fight segregation. Parks enjoyed studying with people of different races and backgrounds. When she returned home, she had a chance to use what she had learned.

In 1955, Parks had a job at a department store in Montgomery. One day, she got on the bus to go home, and she recognized the driver. He was the same man who had ordered her off the bus several years before. This time, Parks took a seat in the middle of the bus. At the next stop, several white people got on, and a white man was left standing.

The bus driver ordered the people in Parks's row to give up their seats. At first, no one stood up. Then everyone but Parks got up. She kept sitting. She was tired after working all day, but no more tired than usual. She was simply tired of giving in.

The bus driver told Parks he would have her arrested. She still did not move. Two police officers came and arrested her. She called home from the police station, and her mother called E. D. Nixon. He came to the station, along with Virginia and Clifford Durr. Her friends paid her bail, and Parks went home.

Then Nixon asked Parks an important question: Would she allow her case to be made a test case against segregation? Parks agreed.

Next Nixon talked with the African American ministers in Montgomery. Nixon told them to ask all African Americans to stop riding the buses. One of the ministers was Martin Luther King, Jr. Nixon asked King to lead the <u>boycott</u> of the buses, and King agreed. A newspaper published a story about the boycott, and black ministers spoke about it in church, urging people not to ride any buses.

African Americans in Montgomery did not ride the buses for over a year. Some went to work in car pools, in wagons, and on horses. Most of them, however, walked. The bus company lost money and had to cut back service. Still, the city did not change its segregation rules.

Some people made threats against the African Americans, and Martin Luther King, Jr.'s house was bombed. African Americans lived in fear, but they continued their boycott. They even persuaded some white people to join them.

Meanwhile, a lawyer named Fred Gray went to court with Rosa Parks for her trial. He entered a plea of not guilty. However, he did not try to defend Parks against the charges. Instead he allowed her to be found guilty so he could then appeal to a higher court.

The United States has many levels of courts. When someone loses a case in a local court, that person can appeal, or ask another court to hear the case all over again. A higher court can then reverse, or change, the decision of the lower court. Gray knew that local courts would not change the segregation laws. The only hope for change was in the higher courts.

In 1956, thirteen months after the bus boycott began, the U.S. Supreme Court settled Parks's case. It was an important victory for all African Americans. The court ruled that segregated buses were unfair. From then on, African Americans in the United States could sit wherever they wished in buses or trains.

Rosa Parks had lost her job in the department store not long after the boycott started. Later she and her family moved to Detroit, Michigan. There she continued to fight for civil rights. She worked in the office of John Conyers, an African American member of Congress. She also served on the board of directors of the NAACP. In 1979, she won an award, the Spingarn Medal, for her civil rights work.

Throughout her long life, Rosa Parks continued working for justice. In 1987, she started the Parks Institute for Self-Development to provide career training for young people. In 1992, she wrote her autobiography, *Rosa Parks: My Story.*

COMPREHENSION

1. Where do the main events in the biography take place?

   _____

   _____

2. In what year was Rosa Parks arrested?

   _____

   _____

3. What did Parks do to cause her arrest?

   _____

   _____

4. How did Virginia Durr help Rosa Parks?

   _____

   _____

5. Tell, in order, what E. D. Nixon did after Rosa Parks was released from jail.

   _____

   _____

   _____

   _____

6. How did the year-long bus boycott affect African Americans?

   _____

   _____

   _____

   _____

7. What was the final effect of Rosa Parks's arrest?

   _____

   _____

   _____

   _____

8. Decide if each statement is true or false. Write *true* or *false* on the line provided.

   _____ a. If a sick child is <u>segregated</u> from other children, she is allowed to sit next to them.

   _____ b. A <u>league</u> could be a group of students who are raising money for citywide recycling bins.

   _____ c. If you <u>boycott</u> a product, you refuse to buy it.

CRITICAL THINKING

1. Rosa Parks was encouraged to believe in herself when she was growing up. Explain how you think this influenced her actions as an adult.

   _____

   _____

   _____

2. Give reasons why you think E. D. Nixon wanted to use Parks's case as a test case against segregation.

   _____

   _____

   _____

3. Explain why you think E. D. Nixon asked Martin Luther King, Jr. to lead the bus boycott.

   _____

   _____

   _____

4. Some white people in Montgomery supported the bus boycott. What does this suggest about these people?

   _____

   _____

   _____

5. Why do you think Rosa Parks lost her job in the department store?

   _____

   _____

   _____

6. Explain why you think Rosa Parks is sometimes called "the mother of the Civil Rights Movement."

   _____

   _____

   _____

SKILL FOCUS: POINT OF VIEW

As you answer these questions, think about how a writer's point of view affects what a reader learns.

1. From what point of view does the narrator tell the story of Rosa Parks's life?

   _____

2. How might the selection have been different if Rosa Parks had told her own life story from the first-person point of view?

   _____

   _____

   _____

3. What might be a strength of a life story written from the third-person point of view?

   _____

   _____

4. Suppose that you were a reporter in 1956. You are writing a news report about the bus boycott. Write the first sentence of your report. Use the third-person point of view.

   _____

Reading-Writing Connection

Suppose you were in Rosa Parks's situation. What would you have said and done when the bus driver ordered you to give up your seat? On a separate sheet of paper, write the conversation that you and the bus driver might have had.

Skill: Differences of Opinion

BACKGROUND INFORMATION

In "Conflict Between the North and the South," you will learn about the differences between the North and the South that led to the American Civil War. The Civil War took more than half a million American lives. The struggle began in April 1861, when Southern troops fired on Fort Sumter in South Carolina. Four years of bloodshed followed. In April 1865, the South surrendered, and the war ended.

SKILL FOCUS: Differences of Opinion

People often disagree about issues and problems. That is because people often look at issues differently. As a result, they draw different conclusions.

Sometimes there are many opinions on an issue. They may all be based on certain facts. Strong arguments can be made to support different opinions on an issue.

It is important to examine **differences of opinion** before drawing your own conclusions on an issue. Here are some questions to ask yourself before you draw conclusions.

- What is the issue on which people disagree?
- How many different opinions are there?
- How are the opinions different?
- What are the reasons for the differences?

▶ Read the sentences below. Then fill in the Opinion Chart in the next column. Write *for* or *against*. Then give your reasons.

People in the North needed good roads to ship their products to other parts of the country. Money to build these roads came from taxes paid by both Northerners and Southerners. The South, however, had many rivers that were good for shipping. Southerners did not need as many roads. Therefore they objected to paying the taxes needed to build roads.

Issue	North	South
Should Southerners have to pay taxes to build roads?	Opinion: Reason:	Opinion: Reason:

CONTEXT CLUES: Using a Dictionary

When there aren't enough context clues to figure out a word's meaning, you need to look up the word in a **dictionary**.

The following sentences give no context clues to the meaning of the underlined word.

The disagreements between the North and the South centered on five major issues. These issues were slavery, <u>tariffs</u>, taxes, power in the House of Representatives, and power in the Senate.

If you look up *tariffs* in a dictionary, you will find that it means "taxes or duties that a government charges on imports and exports."

▶ Look up the meaning of the underlined word in a dictionary. Write its definition on the lines.

After much heated debate, Congress passed the Compromise of 1850. This <u>compromise</u> allowed California to be admitted as a free state.

_____

_____

In the next selection, use a dictionary to find the meanings of *representatives*, *senators*, and *territory*.

> ### Strategy Tip
>
> As you read, think about the differences of opinion that divided the two sections of the nation.

Conflict Between the North and the South

This painting shows the charge of the 54th Massachusetts African American Regiment, on July 18, 1863.

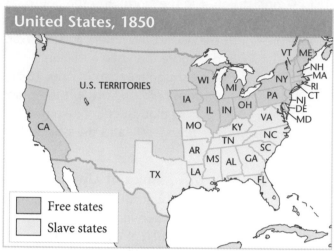

This map shows the United States in 1850, eleven years before the Civil War.

THE CIVIL WAR BEGAN because of many differences between the North and the South. These differences arose in the early 1800s. Tensions grew for several decades. When the war started in 1861, most Americans believed that it would not last long. Instead it stretched into four years of bloody fighting. In the end, more Americans died in the Civil War than in any other war in our history.

The problems the North and the South had centered on five major issues. These issues were slavery, tariffs, taxes, power in the House of Representatives, and power in the Senate. People in the North had strong feelings about these issues. So did people in the South. Each side had reasons for the way it felt.

Slavery

The North and the South had different beliefs about slavery. These beliefs were based on differences in their **economies** (i KAHN ə meez). The economy of a region is the way most people in that area earn their money.

Manufacturing (man yū FAK chər ing) was the most important part of the North's economy. Many people there earned their livings by making things in factories. The North had many workers for its factories because it had a larger population than the South.

The South's economy, on the other hand, was based on **agriculture** (AG rə KUL chər), or growing plants. The most important farms in the South were **plantations** (plan TAY shənz). These were large farms that grew cotton and tobacco. Plantation owners depended on slaves to take care of their huge crops.

Many people in the North did not believe in slavery. They thought the people of the South should not own slaves. Although some Southerners opposed slavery, most believed they needed slaves for their plantations. They said that ending slavery would be a threat to their economy.

Tariffs

Congress has always placed tariffs on manufactured goods imported into the United States. Tariffs raise the price of foreign products. Foreign products then cost more than U.S. products. Northerners liked tariffs. Because of them, more Americans bought cheaper U.S. products made in the North.

Southerners hated tariffs. They needed to sell their cotton in Europe to make money. In exchange, they agreed to buy goods from Europe. Tariffs raised the prices of these European products. That is why Southerners saw tariffs as a kind of tax on them. Their representatives in Congress had argued against tariffs since the early 1800s. However, Congress continued to increase the tariffs.

Taxes

Taxes for road building were also an issue between the North and the South. People in the North needed good roads to ship their products to other parts of the country. Money to build these roads came from taxes paid by both Northerners and Southerners. The South, however, had many rivers that were good for shipping. Southerners used steamboats to ship their crops to the coast. Southerners did not need as many roads. Therefore they objected to paying the taxes needed to build roads. They thought the states should have more say in how to use the money from taxes.

Power in the House of Representatives

Another difference of opinion arose over control of the House of Representatives. In the North, the growing number of factories meant an increasing demand for workers. Many immigrants from Europe settled in the North because of the jobs there. As a result, the population of the North grew quickly. The greater a state's population, the more House representatives it has. Soon the North had more representatives in the House than the South did. This advantage gave Northerners more power to pass laws in the House of Representatives.

The South wanted to have more power in the House. However, its population was smaller than that of the North. Southerners argued for the right to count slaves as part of the population. This way, the South would get more representatives. The North believed that slaves should not be counted just to give Southerners more representatives. In order to count the slaves, the North argued, Southerners must first free them.

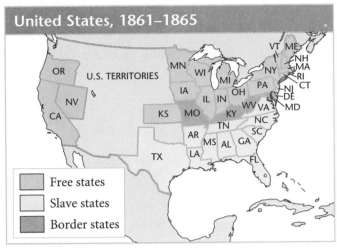

This map shows how the United States was divided during the Civil War.

Power in the Senate

By 1819, there were 15 Northern free states and 15 Southern slave states. Each state had two senators. While the Southerners knew that they could not control the House, they struggled with the North for control of the Senate.

In 1850, the territory of California asked to join the Union as a free state. Northerners favored letting California join the Union. Southerners opposed making California a state. With 16 free states, more senators would come from the North than from the South. If this happened, the free states would gain control of the Senate. After much heated debate, Congress passed the Compromise of 1850. This compromise allowed California to be admitted as a free state. However, the rest of the southwestern territory would be open to slavery if the people who settled there voted for it.

✔ Gradually the tensions between the North and the South grew worse. The Southern states decided that they had no future in the Union and withdrew from it. The country soon divided. In the Civil War that followed, Northerners fought against Southerners. After four years of fighting, the North won the war. The Union was saved. The task of reunion, however, proved to be long and difficult.

Use the maps on pages 96 and 97 to answer questions 1 through 4.

1. How many slave states were in the Union in 1850? _____ by 1865? _____

2. How many free states were in the Union in 1850? _____ by 1865? _____

3. Which four states came into the Union after 1850 as free states? _____

_____

4. How many states were in the Union

   before the war? _____

   after the war? _____

5. List the five major areas of disagreement between the North and the South.

_____

_____

6. Why did the North favor allowing California to enter the Union as a free state?

_____

_____

_____

7. What was the result of the disagreements between the North and the South?

_____

_____

8. Write the letter of the correct meaning on the line next to each word.

   _____ territory

   _____ senators

   _____ representatives

   a. number of members determined by state population

   b. part of the United States that is not a state

   c. members of Congress; two from each state

1. The map on page 97 shows several states as border states. Explain how the conflict might have been different in these states than in other states.

_____

_____

_____

_____

2. Which sentence tells the main idea of the paragraph with a ✔ next to it? Circle the letter next to the correct answer.

   a. The Compromise of 1850 was the main cause of the Civil War.

   b. The disagreements between the North and the South could easily have been resolved.

   c. The differences in interests and viewpoint between the North and the South seemed too great to be settled, and the Civil War resulted.

   d. The Northerners were right all along.

3. Explain why you think most Americans didn't think the Civil War would last very long.

_____

_____

_____

4. State why you think that unifying the country after the war was difficult.

_____

_____

_____

Fill in the chart below by contrasting the opinions expressed in the selection you just read. First read the first column. It identifies the issues on which the two sides had differences of opinion. Next write *For* or *Against* to describe the opinion each side had about the issue. Then write the reason each side had the opinion it did. The first issue is done for you.

Issue	North	South
Slavery	Opinion: *Against* Reason: *Northern factories had enough workers; they didn't need slaves.*	Opinion: *For* Reason: *Cotton and tobacco were the basis of the South's agricultural economy; slaves were used to raise these crops.*
Tariffs on foreign goods	Opinion: Reason:	Opinion: Reason:
Taxes for road construction	Opinion: Reason:	Opinion: Reason:
Inclusion of slaves in population count	Opinion: Reason:	Opinion: Reason:
Admission of California as a free state	Opinion: Reason:	Opinion: Reason:

Reading-Writing Connection

Suppose that you had lived in the United States in 1861. How might you have been affected by the Civil War? On a separate sheet of paper, write a fictional letter to a friend describing the changes the war has made in your life.

Skill: Classifying

BACKGROUND INFORMATION

In "Gems and Other Minerals," you will learn how scientists identify gems and other kinds of minerals. Minerals are the most common solid materials on Earth. The land and oceans, for example, rest on layers of rock made of minerals. Some minerals, such as rock salt, are very common. Other minerals, such as gold and diamonds, are hard to find. The names of minerals often end in the suffix *-ite*. Pencil lead, for example, is *graphite*. Rock salt is *halite*. *Hematite* is our main source of iron.

SKILL FOCUS: Classifying

Grouping similar things together is one way to organize them. This way of organizing things is called **classifying**. For example, a shoe store might classify shoes according to whether they are designed for running, playing basketball, or hiking. By classifying the shoes, the store makes it easier for customers to find the type they need.

Classifying is especially helpful for scientists who work with large numbers of objects. Scientists who study minerals, for example, classify them into groups. The minerals in each group are similar in some ways. They may be similar in color, for example, or in their hardness.

When reading information about groups of objects, ask yourself these questions.

- What is similar about the objects classified together in the same group?
- How are the members of one group different from those of another group?

▸ Think about two minerals you have seen. For example, they could be a diamond and graphite, which is the lead in a pencil. Consider why scientists classify these two minerals in different groups. In the outer circles of the Venn Diagram, list some ways in which the two minerals are different.

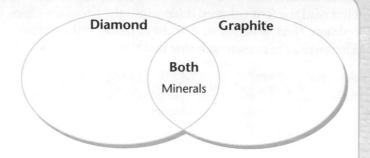

CONTEXT CLUES: Definitions

The context around an unfamiliar word may include a **definition** of the word. The definition tells you the word's meaning. Look for the definition that explains the meaning of the underlined word in the following sentences.

*However, mineralogists have identified all of these minerals. They have arranged them into groups, based on their physical **properties**. A property is a quality or characteristic of a substance.*

The word *properties* is introduced in one sentence and then defined in the next sentence.

▸ Read these sentences from the selection. Circle the definition of *minerals*.

*For thousands of years, people have removed **minerals** from the ground. Minerals do not come from living things or from the remains of living things. Minerals are solid substances found on or in the ground.*

In "Gems and Other Minerals," use definition context clues to find the meanings of the underlined words *texture*, *luster*, and *scale*.

> **Strategy Tip**
>
> As you read "Gems and Other Minerals," look for ways in which the different gems and minerals are alike or different.

Gems and Other Minerals

FOR THOUSANDS OF YEARS, people have removed minerals from the ground. Minerals do not come from living things or from the remains of living things. Minerals are solid substances found on or in the ground.

A gem is a stone that can be cut and polished to make jewelry. Most gems are minerals. Diamonds are minerals, and so are brightly colored gems, such as rubies, sapphires, and emeralds. These four are called **precious** (PRESH əs) stones because they are rare and valuable. They are the most costly gems. Other gems, such as garnets and turquoise, are not as rare or valuable. They are called **semiprecious** (SEM ee PRESH əs) stones.

✔ Iron, copper, talc, gypsum, and aluminum are minerals, too. These minerals, however, are not cut, polished, and used in jewelry. Instead they have many other important uses in construction and industry. Most of these useful minerals are not as valuable as gems.

Some nongem minerals are very valuable and have been used for centuries in jewelry. Gold and silver are two examples of valuable nongem minerals.

The study of minerals is called mineralogy (min ə RAWL ə jee). There are more than 2,000 different kinds of minerals. Many of them look alike. However mineralogists have identified all of these minerals. They have arranged them into groups, based on their **physical properties**. A property is a quality or characteristic of a substance. Physical properties are qualities of a substance that can be identified by one of the five senses. We can see, taste, feel, smell, or hear them.

The physical properties of minerals include color, texture, luster, and hardness.

The most obvious physical property of a mineral is its color. Experts can identify many minerals by color alone. For example, malachite (MAL ə kyt) is always green. Azurite (AZH ə ryt) is always blue.

For centuries, people have valued rare gems for their color and luster.

SCIENCE

Some minerals are the same color. Rubies, for example, are red, as are some kinds of fluorite (FLOR yt) and quartz (kworts). The trained eye of a mineralogist, however, can distinguish the slight color differences of these three minerals.

If scientists cannot identify a mineral by its color, they examine its other physical properties. The way minerals feel, or their <u>texture</u>, can be a clue to their identities. Talc and graphite are greasy to the touch. The clay minerals feel earthy.

Scientists can also identify a mineral by its <u>luster</u>. Luster is the way a mineral reflects light. Some minerals have a dull, or matte, luster. Others are very shiny and are said to have a glassy luster. *Silky*, *pearly*, and *brilliant* are some other words used to describe a mineral's luster.

Hardness is based on which substances can scratch other substances. The blade of a pocket-knife, for example, can scratch a penny. Scientists say that the knife blade is harder than the penny. The same knife blade, though, cannot scratch a diamond. The diamond is harder than the blade.

Mineralogists have made a <u>scale</u>. This is a series of numbers, to show how hard a gem or mineral is. The scale goes from 1 to 10. Talc is rated at 1. It is the softest mineral. Diamonds, the hardest mineral, are rated at 10. Scientists can scratch an unknown mineral sample with tools whose hardnesses are known. Scratching the unknown mineral helps scientists figure out where on the hardness scale the mineral belongs.

A mineral's color, texture, luster, and hardness, as well as other physical properties, determine how it is classified. By testing the physical properties of minerals, a mineralogist can distinguish between minerals that seem alike. Scientists have classified all known minerals.

This open pit copper mine in Utah is one of many that can be found in the United States.

COMPREHENSION

1. Where are minerals found?

   _____

   _____

2. What is a gem?

   _____

   _____

3. What is the difference between precious gems and semiprecious gems?

   _____

   _____

4. What is a physical property?

   _____

   _____

5. What are two nongem minerals that are very valuable?

_____

_____

6. What is the study of minerals called?

_____

_____

7. How many kinds of minerals are there?

_____

_____

8. What are some physical properties of minerals?

_____

_____

9. Complete each sentence with the correct word below.

      scale   texture   luster

a. The _____ of a glass table is smooth.

b. How would you rate her acting on

a _____ of 1 to 10?

c. The wax gave the kitchen floor a

bright _____.

CRITICAL THINKING

1. Explain why it might be important for a jewelry store owner to distinguish between a ruby and a garnet.

_____

2. In the selection, the main idea of the paragraph with a ✔ next to it is not stated. Underline the sentence below that states its main idea.
   a. Some minerals are harder than others.
   b. Some minerals are not gems.
   c. All gems are not minerals.
   d. Gypsum is used to make jewelry.

3. Give reasons why you think mineralogists have arranged minerals into groups, based on their physical properties.

_____

_____

SKILL FOCUS: CLASSIFYING

A. The following chart includes the names of several minerals. Put a ✓ in the correct boxes to show which are gems and which are nongems.

Minerals							
Classification	Diamond	Iron	Emerald	Garnet	Gypsum	Copper	Talc
Gem							
Nongem							

B. Complete the following chart. Put a ✓ in the correct boxes to show which gems are precious and which are semiprecious.

Gems						
Classification	Diamond	Garnet	Sapphire	Emerald	Turquoise	Ruby
Precious						
Semiprecious						

C. Use the following chart to answer the questions below it.

Precious Gems				
Property	Diamond	Sapphire	Ruby	Emerald
Hardness	10	9	9	8
Color	usually colorless	usually blue	red	green

1. Which is harder, a diamond or a sapphire? _____

2. Which is harder, a sapphire or an emerald? _____

3. What color is a ruby? _____

D. Use the following chart to answer the questions below it.

Mohs Hardness Scale										
Mineral	Talc	Gypsum	Calcite	Fluorite	Apatite	Feldspar	Quartz	Topaz	Corundum	Diamond
Hardness	1	2	3	4	5	6	7	8	9	10

1. Which mineral is hardest? _____

2. Which mineral is softest? _____

3. Which is harder, feldspar or quartz? _____

4. Which is harder, topaz or corundum? _____

5. Which is harder, calcite or fluorite? _____

Reading-Writing Connection

Which gems or other minerals can you identify at home, around your community, or in a jewelry store? On a separate sheet of paper, list at least five minerals you find, and describe their color, texture, luster, and hardness.

Skill: Word Problems

BACKGROUND INFORMATION

In this math selection, you will learn how to solve word problems that require two steps or operations. Many familiar tasks have two main steps. For example, you wash you clothes first and then you dry them. You outline a report first and then you write it. In the same way, many math problems also have two main steps. You have to decide on the two arithmetic operations and then complete them before you can solve the word problem.

SKILL FOCUS: Word Problems

Word problems are math problems that are described in sentences. The sentences include all the information you need to solve the problem. Sometimes you will need to do more than one arithmetic operation to solve a word problem. You might have to add and then multiply.

Follow these five steps to solve word problems with two operations.

1. **Read the problem.** Think about the question that is being asked. In your mind, picture the information you are given, or draw an actual picture of it. If necessary, reread the problem. Be sure that you know what the labels used with each number mean.

2. **Decide how to find the answer.** Do you need to add, subtract, multiply, or divide? Think about whether you will need to do one operation or two operations to get the answer. Then write the one or two mathematical sentences that will give you the answer.

3. **Estimate the answer.** Make an educated guess about the answer, based on the information given. Use rounded numbers to make your estimate. If two operations are needed, estimate the answers to both.

4. **Carry out the plan.** Solve the first mathematical sentence you have written. Then solve the second one. Usually you will need the answer from the first operation to solve the second one.

5. **Reread the problem.** Then write the complete answer. Does your answer to the problem make sense? How close is it to your estimate?

▶ Read this word problem. Then answer the question below.

Jake earned $65 last week. He spent $25 on a pair of jeans. Then he gave half of what he had left to his sister for a birthday present. How much money did Jake give his sister?

What two arithmetic operations will solve this problem?

_____

WORD CLUES

When you read word problems, look for the words that signal which operations to use. In two-step problems, you should look for the **signal words** for both operations. Words such as *and*, *total*, *all together*, and *twice as much* tell you that the answer will be larger than the numbers in the problem. To find the answer, you will usually have to add or multiply.

Signal words such as *how much more*, *left*, *each*, and *divided* tell you that your answer will be less than at least one of the numbers in the problem. Often you will either subtract or divide to find the answer.

▶ Circle the words in this problem that signal you to add and then divide.

Juanita ran 1,600 yards on Monday and 1,200 yards on Tuesday. In all, this was 7 laps around the track. How many yards is each lap?

Strategy Tip

Read each problem in "Solving Word Problems With Two Operations." Remember to look for signal words that may help you decide which operations to use.

Solving Word Problems With Two Operations

These are the five steps that you can use to solve word problems.

1. Read the problem.
2. Decide how to find the answer.
3. Estimate the answer.
4. Carry out the plan.
5. Reread the problem.

When working with problems that require two operations, you will need to decide which two operations are necessary to find the answer. It may help to draw a picture or a diagram. When you estimate, you will need to estimate the answers to both arithmetic operations. When you carry out the plan, you will need to do two arithmetic operations to solve the problem.

Use the five steps to solve the problem below.

Read the Problem

Before the Battle of Fort Sumter in 1861, Major Anderson reported that this much food was left: 6 barrels of flour, 3 barrels of sugar, and 24 barrels of salt pork. How many more barrels of salt pork were there than the total barrels of flour and sugar?

Read the problem again. Be sure that you know the label that is used with each number fact. Are there any words that you do not know? If so, look them up to find their meanings. What question does the problem ask? Often the question is asked in the last sentence. *How many more barrels of salt pork were there than the total barrels of flour and sugar?*

Decide How to Find the Answer

You will need to do two arithmetic operations to find the answer. The problem tells you that there are 24 barrels of salt pork. You need to first find out how much flour and sugar there are combined. For the first operation, you must add because you are combining amounts. The key word *total* in the last

sentence of the problem is the clue to add. The following is your mathematical sentence.

$$6 + 3 = n$$

For the second operation, you must subtract because you are comparing the number of barrels of salt pork with the number of barrels of flour and sugar taken together. The key words *how many more* give the clue to subtract. The following is your mathematical sentence.

$$24 - n = b$$

In this mathematical sentence, the letter n stands for the answer to the first operation. When you need to use another letter, you can choose the first letter of the label in the problem. The letter b stands for the difference between the number of *barrels* of flour and sugar combined and the number of *barrels* of salt pork.

Estimate the Answer

Use rounded numbers to make an estimate. Round to the nearest ten, first adding and then subtracting.

First operation: $6 + 3 = 9$
Round to 10.
Second operation: $20 - 10 = 10$
Your estimate is 10.

Carry Out the Plan

Do the arithmetic.
First operation: $6 + 3 = 9$
Second operation: $24 - 9 = 15$

Reread the Problem

After rereading the problem, write the complete answer. *There were 15 more barrels of salt pork than there were total barrels of flour and sugar.* Does the answer make sense? How close is your answer to your estimate? If the answer is not close to your estimate, you should start all over.

Use the five steps to solve this problem.

Read: *General Sherman commanded 100,000 soldiers. He divided them into two equal groups. Then 12,500 more soldiers joined one of the groups. What was the total number of soldiers in the larger group?*

Decide: You will need to do two operations to solve this problem. The problem describes a large group: 100,000. For the first operation, you must break this group into two smaller groups. The key word *divided* is a clue to divide. For the second operation, you must combine two number facts. The word *total* is a clue to add. Write a mathematical sentence for each step.

$$100,000 \div 2 = n$$
$$n + 12,500 = s$$

The letter *s* stands for the total number of soldiers in the larger group.

Estimate: Round the larger numbers to the nearest ten thousand. Then divide and add.

$$100,000 \div 2 = 50,000$$
$$50,000 + 10,000 = 60,000$$

Carry Out:

$$100,000 \div 2 = 50,000$$
$$50,000 + 12,500 = 62,500$$

Reread: After rereading the question, write the complete answer. *There were 62,500 soldiers in the larger group.* Does this answer make sense? How close is it to your estimate?

COMPREHENSION

1. List the five steps for solving word problems.

   a. _____

   b. _____

   c. _____

   d. _____

   e. _____

2. **a.** What label is used in the first problem in the selection? _____

   b. What label is used in the second problem in the selection? _____

3. Sometimes two operations are needed to solve a problem. List the three steps in which you would have to do the two operations.

   a. _____

   b. _____

   c. _____

CRITICAL THINKING

1. Explain why you should start all over if your answer is not close to your estimate.

   _____

   _____

2. Explain how drawing a picture of the information that is given can help you solve a word problem.

   _____

   _____

   _____

3. In a problem that requires two operations, explain why you can't do the second operation first.

   _____

   _____

4. Tell why you use two different letters to stand for the numbers you are looking for.

   _____

   _____

MATHEMATICS

Use the five steps to solve these word problems.

1. **Read:** The soldiers at Fort Sumter had 6 barrels of flour and 2 barrels of vinegar. A shipment of food to the fort contained twice as much food as they already had. What was the total number of barrels in the shipment?

   Decide: _____

   Estimate: _____

   Carry Out: _____

   Reread: _____

2. **Read:** By the end of the Civil War, about 800,000 soldiers had served in the Confederate Army. Of these, 258,000 had died and 225,000 had been wounded. How many Confederate soldiers were left neither dead nor wounded?

   Decide: _____

   Estimate: _____

   Carry Out: _____

   Reread: _____

3. **Read:** General Schofield marched 18 miles with his soldiers. It took them 6 hours. About how many hours would it take to march 24 miles?

   Decide: _____

   _____

   Estimate: _____

   Carry Out: _____

   Reread: _____

Reading-Writing Connection

On a separate sheet of paper, describe an occasion when you have had to use two mathematical operations to solve a problem. Write down the five steps you followed to solve the problem.

Skill: Syllables

The following is a summary of rules to help you divide words into **syllables**.

RULE 1. In a compound word, divide between the two smaller words.

RULE 2. In words with double consonants, divide between the double consonants.

RULE 3. In words with a prefix or suffix, divide between the base word and its prefix or suffix.

RULE 4. In words with two consonants between two sounded vowels, divide between the two consonants.

RULE 5a. In words with one consonant between two sounded vowels with the first vowel long, you usually divide before the consonant.

RULE 5b. In words with one consonant between two sounded vowels with the first vowel short, you usually divide after the consonant.

RULE 6. Do not divide between consonant blends or consonant and *-le*. Consider a consonant blend as if it were one consonant.

Divide each of the words below into two syllables. Write the syllables separately on the line to the right of the word. Then write the number of the rule or rules that you used on the line to the left of the word. If two or more different rules apply to the same word, write all the rule numbers that you used for the word. The first word is done for you.

1. ___1___ gangplank _____gang plank_____

2. _____ luggage _____

3. _____ rainfall _____

4. _____ market _____

5. _____ doorway _____

6. _____ chemist _____

7. _____ shoulder _____

8. _____ cobble _____

9. _____ polar _____

10. _____ coastal _____

11. _____ careful _____

12. _____ unkind _____

13. _____ fever _____

14. _____ porridge _____

15. _____ candle _____

16. _____ fertile _____

17. _____ cyclone _____

18. _____ enter _____

19. _____ moonstone _____

20. _____ limestone _____

21. _____ turkey _____

22. _____ linen _____

23. _____ steamer _____

24. _____ yearly _____

25. _____ battle _____

26. _____ carbon _____

27. _____ motion _____

28. _____ captain _____

If someone told you that Muscles Malone was the greatest wrestler in history, you might agree with the statement or you might not agree. That is because the statement is an opinion. It is not a statement of fact.

There is a big difference between a fact and an opinion. A statement of **fact** can be checked and proven. If you hear or read that city hall has just been painted, you can look at city hall to see the new coat of paint. If you hear or read that a certain football team won all their games in 1995, you can check a record book. A statement of fact can be proved by checking other sources.

A statement of **opinion** tells what someone believes or feels. Such statements as "The Peanuts are the best team in the state" or "Dancing Danny is a better wrestler than Muscles Malone" are opinions.

It is difficult to prove or disprove statements of opinion. Words such as *better, best, worse,* and *worst* are sometimes found in opinions. These words do not mean the same thing to everyone.

There is nothing wrong with opinions. Everyone has them, and it's interesting to share your opinions with other people. Look at these two statements.

1. The Bulldogs are the best baseball team in the league.
2. The Bulldogs have won 25 out of 30 games this year.

Which statement would you accept as a fact? The second one is a fact because it is based on information that can be checked.

When you hear or read statements such as these, you need to decide whether they are facts or opinions.

Read the following statements. Some are statements of facts. Others are statements of opinions. On the line before each statement, write *F* if it is a fact or *O* if it is an opinion.

1. The Somerset Street team has the best swimmers.
2. The Somerset Street team won first place in three races.
3. Harry Sandler ran the mile in 3 minutes, 59 seconds.
4. Bill Jamal is better looking than Sam Sorensen.
5. Pam Choi jogs every morning from six o'clock to eight o'clock.
6. Larry Johnson is taller than Charlie Sanchez.
7. The next world champion will be chosen on December 15.
8. Carla threw her tennis racket to the ground.
9. Mike is a poor loser.
10. Sahar is the best tennis player on the team.
11. The first team to score five points wins the match.
12. The Wildcats are a better team than the Cougars.
13. It is wrong to have ball games on Saturday nights.
14. The Strawtown Champions play the Tor Terrors every other Saturday.
15. Surely there are better ways to spend a Saturday night.
16. Tracy has been on the Tor Terrors team for three years.

Skill: Similes and Metaphors

Sometimes an author compares two things that are not really alike. An author does this to draw a sharp picture in the reader's mind. These comparisons make what you are reading more interesting and colorful.

Read the following sentences.
Heather looks good in her new coat.
Heather looks like a million dollars in her new coat.

Which of the two sentences above gives a clearer, more interesting picture of how Heather looks? If you said the second one, you are right. In this sentence, a girl is being compared to a million dollars. Comparing two unlike things using the word *like* or *as* is called a **simile**.

Read the following sentences.
During August, the room was an oven.
During August, the room was hot.

Which sentence gives a better idea of how hot the room was? The first sentence does. This sentence contains a **metaphor**. A metaphor, like a simile, compares two unlike things, but neither *like* nor *as* is used. A metaphor compares two things by suggesting that one thing is really another. A room and an oven are not usually alike, except in this special way—both are hot.

To understand a sentence that uses either a simile or a metaphor, you need to decide which two things are being compared. Then you can use context clues to figure out the way in which the two unlike things are similar.

Underline the two things being compared in each sentence. Then fill in the circle next to the sentence that explains the meaning of the simile or metaphor.

1. At the campfire, I felt as snug as a bug in a rug.
   ○ A bug was in my clothes.
   ○ I felt warm and comfortable.

2. Mr. Filbert's living room is a greenhouse.
   ○ The living room is filled with plants.
   ○ The living room is painted green.

3. The baby is growing like a weed.
   ○ The baby is growing quickly.
   ○ The weeds in the garden are small.

4. Doctor Rodriquez is as gentle as a lamb.
   ○ Doctor Rodriquez takes care of lambs.
   ○ Doctor Rodriquez is calm and patient.

5. Clouds are cotton balls in the sky.
   ○ Clouds look soft and white.
   ○ Cotton balls are in the sky.

6. Steven eats like a horse.
   ○ Steven eats a lot of food.
   ○ Steven eats hay.

7. Amy ran as fast as a deer.
   ○ Amy liked to run with deer.
   ○ Amy ran at a fast pace.

8. Dewdrops sparkled like diamonds on the grass.
   ○ Dewdrops and diamonds were on the grass.
   ○ The grass was shiny from dew.

9. Sarah told Jack to stop working like a horse.
   ○ Jack was working too hard.
   ○ Jack was working in a field of grass.

10. At high noon, the desert is like a furnace.
    ○ The desert is used for burning trash.
    ○ The desert is very hot.

Skill: Using a Table of Contents

Using a **table of contents** saves you time when you want to find out what kind of information is in a book. The table of contents gives you a quick overview of the chapters and topics in the book.

It lists the titles of the chapters and gives the page on which each chapter begins. Sometimes a table of contents also lists the most important topics included in each chapter. It may even give the page on which each topic begins.

To use a table of contents, glance through the chapter titles and topics until you find the subject you want to read about. Then turn to the page number given next to the chapter title or topic. Read this section until you find the information you need on your subject.

Below is a table of contents from a science book. To answer the questions on page 113, use these two steps.

1. Look at the chapter titles to find out under which one you might find the information asked for.

2. Read through the topics under that title to find out on which page that particular topic begins.

CONTENTS

1. You need to find information about trout.

   a. Under which chapter title would you look? _____

   b. Under which topic would you look? _____

   c. On which page would you start to read? _____

2. You need to find information about thunderstorms.

   a. Under which chapter title would you look? _____

   b. Under which topic would you look? _____

   c. On which page would you start to read? _____

3. You need to find information about how to improve garden soil.

   a. Under which chapter title would you look? _____

   b. Under which topic would you look? _____

   c. On which page would you start to read? _____

4. You need to find information about how minerals are formed.

   a. Under which chapter title would you look? _____

   b. Under which topic would you look? _____

   c. On which page would you start to read? _____

5. You need to find information about the use of the mineral calcium.

   a. Under which chapter title would you look? _____

   b. Under which topic would you look? _____

   c. On which page would you start to read? _____

6. You need to find information about air pressure.

   a. Under which chapter title would you look? _____

   b. Under which topic would you look? _____

   c. On which page would you start to read? _____

7. You need to find information about reptiles.

   a. Under which chapter title would you look? _____

   b. Under which topic would you look? _____

   c. On which page would you start to read? _____

8. You need to find information about the causes of snow.

   a. Under which chapter title would you look? _____

   b. Under which topic would you look? _____

   c. On which page would you start to read? _____

Skill: Alphabetical Order

In a dictionary, you often find several pages of words that all begin with the same two letters. To find a word on these pages, you will need to use the third letter of the word. For example, the word *fabric* is listed before the word *face* because *b* comes before *c* in the alphabet. When words begin with the same two letters, they are arranged in **alphabetical order** according to the third letter in the words.

A. On the numbered lines, write each set of words below in alphabetical order according to the first three letters in each word. Cross out each word in the list after you write it.

lodge   1. _____   seize   1. _____

long   2. _____   serve   2. _____

loan   3. _____   self   3. _____

love   4. _____   sew   4. _____

loft   5. _____   set   5. _____

loom   6. _____   secret   6. _____

lock   7. _____   seven   7. _____

log   8. _____   senior   8. _____

lose   9. _____   seal   9. _____

low   10. _____   seed   10. _____

Sometimes you will need to use the fourth letter of a word in order to find the word in the dictionary. The word *honey* is listed before the word *honor* because *e* comes before *o* in the alphabet. When words begin with the same three letters, they are arranged in alphabetical order according to the fourth letter in the words.

B. On the numbered lines, write each set of words below in alphabetical order according to the first four letters in each word. Cross out each word in the list after you write it.

collar   1. _____   merge   1. _____

column   2. _____   merry   2. _____

color   3. _____   mercy   3. _____

cold   4. _____   merit   4. _____

colt   5. _____   mere   5. _____

Skill: Dewey Decimal System

Call numbers on library books tell you exactly where each book is kept in a library. A call number is found on the spine, or narrow back edge, of the book, and on each card in the card catalog or each entry in the computer catalog. The call number is determined by the subject of the book. Books on the same subject have similar call numbers and are kept in the same section of the library.

In most libraries, books are classified according to the **Dewey Decimal System**. It is called a decimal system because books are classified according to ten general subject areas.

Study the numbers and subjects of the Dewey Decimal System.

Main Classes of the Dewey Decimal System		
Numbers	**Subject**	**Examples of Types of Books**
000–099	General Reference Works	encyclopedias, bibliographies
100–199	Philosophy and Behavior	conduct, morals
200–299	Religion	myths, Bible, religious beliefs
300–399	Social Science	law, customs
400–499	Languages	dictionaries, English and foreign languages
500–599	Pure Science	astronomy, chemistry, biology
600–699	Applied Science	engineering, radio, space flight
700–799	Arts and Recreation	music, sports, paintings
800–899	Literature	plays, poems
900–999	History	geography, biography, history

Suppose you are studying the Civil War. In which number category would you find books on this subject? Since the Civil War is classified as history, Civil War books are found in the 900s. After locating the subject card in the card catalog, you see that the call number for Civil War books is 973. Libraries usually label each section of shelves so you can find a book easily.

On the line next to each type of book below, write the number category in which you would find it.

1. a book that teaches French _____

2. a book explaining how to ski _____

3. an encyclopedia article on Mexico _____

4. a book comparing religions _____

5. a book describing discoveries in astronomy, such as quasars and black holes _____

6. the plays of Shakespeare _____

7. a book about how people behave at work _____

8. a book about the laws of the United States _____

9. a book explaining how rocket engines work _____

10. a book about Viking explorers _____

Skill: Reading a Television Schedule

What is the easiest way to find out what shows are on television? Check a newspaper schedule or a local program guide. A **television schedule** shows what time each program begins and what channel it is on. The schedule may give a brief summary of some programs, as well as other information. Many schedules list programs on cable or satellite television. These programs are listed after the regular television shows.

Examine the following television schedule.

Wednesday Evening

7:00 **2** NEWS UPDATE

4 NIGHTLY NEWS

5 ALL AROUND THE U.S.A. Variety Singer Mary Aruba entertains in Southern cities, including Charleston, Atlanta, and New Orleans.

7 LOCAL NEWS REPORT

9 MOVIE Drama "Soldier Boys" (1988) Three boys leave their homes for the first time to enlist in the Civil War. Mark Simon, Carl Bianco, Alan Peters. (90 min.)

11 DERECHO DE NACER

13 BUSINESS NEWS

WAT PEOPLE ON THE MOVE Travel

7:05 **2** BASEBALL Greenville Tigers / Mason City Bulldogs at Mason City

7:30 **4** MOPPETS Children

7 WORLDWIDE NEWS

11 LUIS AND FRIENDS Interview Host Luis Raphael talks to basketball star Kirk Stratton and 12-year-old actress Lindsay Gray.

13 BLUEGRASS FESTIVAL Music performances by Smoky Mountain Singers, Billy Joe Flynn, Rita Murray.

HPO BIG JOE DANIELS Country Music

ESN SPORTS Pro Volleyball

8:00 **4** AUTO RACING The Meadowbrook 200, taped April 20. (30 min.)

5 TV MAGAZINE Tips on hair care; a group of students model Civil War fashions they created.

7 MOVIE Drama "Attack" (1992) When President Lincoln (Spencer Flack) sends troops to Fort Sumter, they are forced to surrender, and the Confederate flag is raised. (2 hrs.)

11 ONE COUPLE Comedy Guest Sandy Newman plays a nervous runner in her first marathon.

13 DANCE TODAY The Downtown Ballet Company performs "Steps in Time."

WLM MOVIE Musical "High School Prom." (1972) Hilariously funny. Todd Michaels at his best.

8:30 **4** GYMNASTICS National High School Tournament, taped May 1 in Chicago. (60 min.)

5 NORTH AND SOUTH Drama During the second battle of Bull Run. Union General Pope (Frank Courtney) is outwitted by Generals Lee and Jackson. (2 hrs.)

11 INCREDIBLE DAYS Drama Roger (Jeff Lynch) plays an astronaut captured by the inhabitants of an alien planet. (Repeat; 60 min.)

13 GUESS WHAT? Game Show

HPO MOVIE Drama "Office Politics" (2000) Modern-day drama about two best friends who want the same job.

ESN SPORTS Pro Curling National Championships Live from Appleton Center. (2 hrs.)

A. Circle the letter of the phrase that completes each sentence below. Use the information on the television schedule on page 116.

1. Two programs scheduled at 7:00 include
   a. "News Update" on Channel 2 and "Rocco's Kitchen" on Channel 62.
   b. "Worldwide News" on Channel 7 and "All Around the U.S.A." on Channel 5.
   c. "Worldwide News" on Channel 7 and "Auto Racing" on Channel 4.
   d. "News Update" on Channel 2 and "Local News Report" on Channel 7.

2. On "TV Magazine," you will learn about
   a. hair care and clothing worn during the Civil War period.
   b. a basketball star and a teenage actress.
   c. Charleston, Atlanta, and New Orleans.
   d. the Downtown Ballet Company.

3. A baseball game between the Tigers and Bulldogs
   a. begins at 7:00.
   b. begins at 7:05.
   c. begins at 7:30.
   d. begins at 8:00.

4. The number 1998 following the title of the 7:00 movie means that this movie
   a. will be aired 1998 times.
   b. was last shown on television in 1998.
   c. was first shown on television in 1998.
   d. was made in 1998.

5. If you want to see a movie and laugh and sing, you should watch
   a. "Soldier Boys."
   b. "Office Politics."
   c. "High School Prom."
   d. "Attack."

6. The only sports show on cable television between 7:00 and 8:30 is
   a. baseball.
   b. gymnastics.
   c. volleyball.
   d. basketball.

B. Decide if each of the following questions can be answered using the television schedule on page 116. Write *yes* or *no* on each line.

1. Which programs are on at 6:00 P.M.? _____

2. At what time is "One Couple" over? _____

3. Does Spencer Flack star in the movie "Attack"? _____

4. On what channel is "Business News"? _____

5. On what date did the Meadowbrook 200 auto race take place? _____

6. Who are the finalists in the gymnastics tournament? _____

7. What is "Derecho de Nacer" about? _____

8. Are any programs for children scheduled on Wednesday night? _____

9. Is "Luis and Friends" a live or a taped program? _____

10. What is the name of the game show host on "Guess What"? _____

Mexico

LESSON 41

Skill: Theme

BACKGROUND INFORMATION

"Life Goes On" is about a real-life Mexican family whose way of life is threatened when a volcano erupts in a nearby town. On February 20, 1943, a Mexican farmer felt the earth tremble as he plowed his cornfield. Smoke and lava began flowing from a crack in the earth beneath his plow. That lava gave birth to a new volcano that soon rose over 300 feet (90 meters) high. The volcano was named Parícutin (par EE koo teen), the name of a nearby village. Lava flowing from the volcano slowly buried Parícutin and other nearby villages.

SKILL FOCUS: Theme

Theme is the meaning or message of a story. It is an idea about life that the author wants readers to understand. Often the theme is a general statement about life or people, such as "If you try to please everyone, you'll end up pleasing no one." Sometimes an author states the theme of a story directly. Other times, the theme is not stated. Then the reader has to infer, or figure out, the theme.

You can figure out a story's theme by paying attention to what the characters do and say. The story's title may also be a clue to its theme. The following questions will help you infer the theme.

- What does the story's title mean?
- What do the main characters discover about themselves in the story?
- What do the characters learn about life?
- What message is the author giving to readers?

▶ Many books and movies have similar themes. In the chart in the next column, there are two common themes. Complete the chart with the name of a book or movie you know that conveys each theme.

Theme	Book or Movie
If you keep trying and never give up, your dreams may come true.	
Sometimes a tragedy brings people together and strengthens their love.	

CONTEXT CLUES: Details

Some context clues are **details**. Details help show the meaning of a new word. In the sentence below, look for details that explain the meaning of *billowed*.

Then in Parícutin, a town about 15 miles (24 kilometers) away, a tower of smoke and steam rose from the earth and **billowed** *high into the sky.*

If you don't know the meaning of *billowed*, the details in the sentence can help you figure it out. These details tell you that a great deal of smoke and steam rose into the air. If you can picture that scene, you might be able to guess that *billowed* means "rose in big swelling waves."

▶ Read the following sentence. Circle the details that help you figure out the meaning of the underlined word.

A **barrage** *of burning stones clattered down, bombarding anyone who went too close.*

Use detail context clues to find the meanings of the underlined words *feverishly*, *spindly*, and *abundant* in "Life Goes On."

⎛ Strategy Tip ⎞

As you read "Life Goes On," think about the story's theme. Use the questions on this page to help you figure it out.

Life Goes On

"Today we will plow the cornfield," Mr. Gutiérrez announced to his sons one February morning. Luis obediently went to yoke the oxen. Pedro, however, made a face and muttered, "What's the use?"

"What's the use?" Mr. Gutiérrez repeated. The question seemed strange to him. "Since the ancient times," he said, "our people have plowed this land. We have always planted corn. It is the way we live. The corn did not grow last year, but it is sure to grow this year. Life must go on."

Pedro thought back to last February and the events that had changed their lives. For days, the earth had trembled. Then in Parícutin, a town about 15 miles (24 kilometers) away, a tower of smoke and steam rose from the earth and billowed high into the sky.

When the sun rose the next day, a 10-meter (33-foot) mound of lava had formed in the field. Smoke and ash were surging upward. A barrage of burning stones clattered down, bombarding anyone who went too close. By week's end, the hill of fire was 50 meters (164 feet) high and still growing.

Lava from the volcano swallowed the village of Parícutin. Ash and cinders rained down. Meter by meter, the sea of lava flowed across the countryside. It even buried the town of San Juan Parangaricutiro. Only the top of the town's church tower could still be seen poking through the lava. For months, people fleeing from the buried villages passed through Uruapan, the town near Pedro's home.

"Will the lava bury Uruapan?" Pedro asked his father. "Will we have to leave our home, too?" A thick layer of ash already coated their land.

"No, we will be safe here," Pedro's father announced, as if he knew the mind of the volcano. "Our life will go on as before."

In a way, Mr. Gutiérrez was right. The Parícutin volcano finally stopped erupting. The forces of fire retreated into the earth. The flow of lava stopped. Life, however, did not go on as before.

Day and night, Pedro's family worked <u>feverishly</u> to clear ash and cinders from their fields in time to plant. They worked without stopping, desperate to save the land they loved, the land that gave them life.

Later, with high hopes, they placed the corn seeds in the soil. The rains came, and the seeds sprouted. For a while, the bright green seedlings gave them hope.

That hope did not last, though. After a month, the corn stopped growing. The short, <u>spindly</u> stalks turned brown. The stalks were too thin and weak to grow much corn. The small, half-formed ears of corn that finally appeared were worthless. Something in the ash had destroyed the crop.

Since then, a year had passed. Now Pedro's father was asking him to hope for the best again. Pedro watched his brother Luis lead the yoke of oxen to the field. Mr. Gutiérrez had the plow. For the next few weeks, they would plow and replow the soil. Then they would plant their seeds.

What if the corn didn't grow again this year? Pedro couldn't bear to think about it. He felt as if he couldn't even watch his father and brother work. Throwing the saddle onto his father's horse, he galloped toward Uruapan.

Meanwhile, news of the Parícutin volcano had spread around the world. This was the first time in recorded history that a volcano had been born. Scientists came to study the new volcano. Curious tourists visited it, too. They wanted to explore the lava beds. They wanted to see the top of the church tower poking through the sea of lava. To get there from Uruapan, however, they needed guides.

"Could you guide me over the lava beds to the Parícutin volcano?" a man asked Pedro. "I want to see the volcano and the buried village."

Pedro had been to the volcano twice with Luis. He knew the path well enough. He nodded to the tourist. He would be the man's guide.

Pedro helped the man rent a horse. Then they rode out together across the hardened lava. Sometimes the man would reach out and touch a rock that had formed from the lava. Pedro smiled. The man acted as if it might still be hot. Pedro

pointed out the strange sight of the church tower, poking through a sea of jagged volcanic rock. Finally they saw the smoking crater of Parícutin. Back in Uruapan, the man handed Pedro 300 pesos. It was more money than Pedro had ever had.

It was dark when Pedro got home. "Where did you ride off to?" Pedro's father asked. He wasn't angry, only worried.

Pedro told his family about the tourist in Uruapan. He described his trip across the lava bed. Then he gave his father the 300 pesos.

"Many tourists are coming to Uruapan to see the volcano," Pedro told his father. "They will pay guides to lead them there." Then Pedro turned to his mother. "The tourists like to buy blankets in the market. If you weave blankets, we can sell them."

"There is no time for weaving now," Mrs. Gutiérrez said. "We have to plant and hoe the cornfields. Life must go on."

Pedro stared out at the ashy fields. "The volcano has changed our life," he said at last. "We cannot continue in the same old ways."

From then on, Pedro helped his father and Luis in the cornfields on some days. On other days, he worked as a guide to the volcano. Pedro gave some of his earnings to his parents. He used the rest to buy another horse.

At home, the corn seeds sprouted. For a while, the young plants grew well. Then, just as in the previous year, the stalks stopped growing. The ears of corn were tiny and only half-formed. It would be another disastrous harvest.

Mrs. Gutiérrez began to spend more time at her loom. She was weaving blankets and shawls. Mr. Gutiérrez and Luis helped her work. They cleaned and spun wool. They had never done that before.

By the end of the summer, Pedro had two horses and two saddles. He took them to Uruapan often. He was one of the best guides in the area. Some tourists even asked for him by name.

On Wednesdays, Mrs. Gutiérrez rode to Uruapan with her son. He had rented her a stall at the marketplace. There she spread out her colorful blankets and shawls. The tourists loved her work.

The months went by. Although the corn crop had failed, the family had enough to eat. Pedro and his mother had earned money to buy corn and other food. There was money to buy other things, too.

When it was planting time again, Mr. Gutiérrez spent a day walking through his fields. "Next week, we will start to plow," he announced to his sons.

Pedro rolled his eyes. "Why should we plow the land and plant corn?" he finally asked. "What's the use?"

"Life must go on," Mr. Gutiérrez replied.

"The corn does not grow here anymore," Pedro protested. "Our life must change."

Mr. Gutiérrez sighed. "The corn will grow this year," he said at last.

Luis nodded and went out to work on the plow. Pedro shook his head and went out to feed his horses. Tomorrow he would guide tourists to the volcano. With any luck, he would be able to forget about his father's foolish hope for a corn crop.

As it turned out, however, the corn crop was very much on Pedro's mind. The tourists that day were from Mexico City. One of them, Professor Zedillo, taught agriculture there. "Are farmers still able to grow corn where you live?" he asked Pedro. "Or is there too much volcanic ash in the soil?"

Pedro told the sad story of his family's last two harvests. He described the brown cornstalks and the half-formed ears of corn. "Now my father and brother are ready to plow again," Pedro concluded. "I suspect it will all be for nothing."

"You're probably right, Pedro," Professor Zedillo

agreed. "Probably no corn will grow on your land for many years, unless you use subsoil plows."

"Subsoil plows?" Pedro asked.

"Plows that cut deep into the ground," the professor explained. "That way, the deep soil gets plowed up to the surface, and the ash gets buried. Oxen aren't able to pull subsoil plows, though. You need a tractor."

"My family could never afford a tractor and subsoil plows," Pedro said, shaking his head.

"The university is doing some experiments with subsoil plowing in areas around Uruapan this month," the professor replied. "Maybe your farm could be part of the experiment."

Two weeks later, a tractor rumbled down the road toward the Gutiérrez's land. It was the first tractor the family had ever seen. The tractor pulled a giant set of plows. Each blade on the plows was taller than Pedro.

With a belch of black smoke, the tractor roared into action. The gleaming subsoil plows sliced deep into the ancient soil. Around and around the field

went the tractor, leaving a trail of deep furrows. By the end of the day, the fields were ready for planting.

That February, Pedro spent less time guiding tourists. Instead he helped his father and Luis with the crops. Pedro had bought the best seed he could find in Uruapan. When the tiny green fingers of corn broke through the soil, joy filled his heart.

March passed and April came. The corn continued to grow well. The thick stalks stayed bright green. They supported many ears of corn. The ears were long and full of kernels. The harvest would be an <u>abundant</u> one.

At harvest, the whole family worked together, cutting the corn and loading the ears into a cart. Together they picked out the best ears to save for next year.

"This will be our seed corn, the seeds we plant next year," Mr. Gutiérrez said. "Life must go on."

Pedro stared out at the cornfield, thinking about the year that had just passed. "Yes, father, you are right," he said. "One way or another, life goes on."

COMPREHENSION

1. Where does this story take place?

_____

_____

2. How does the volcano at Parícutin affect the Gutiérrez family?

_____

_____

3. Compare how Pedro and Luis react when their father decides to plant corn again each year.

_____

_____

4. How does Pedro help his family?

_____

_____

5. Explain why Mrs. Gutiérrez starts going to Uruapan on Wednesdays.

_____

_____

6. Fill in the circle next to the synonym for each word.

   a. feverishly
      ○ foolishly   ○ desperately   ○ easily

   b. spindly
      ○ thin   ○ annoying   ○ disappointing

   c. abundant
      ○ few   ○ plentiful   ○ unnecessary

1. Discuss how Pedro shows that he is different from his father.

   _____

   _____

2. Explain why a tractor comes to plow the fields at Pedro's farm.

   _____

   _____

3. Discuss some lessons about life that Pedro learns during the story.

   _____

   _____

SKILL FOCUS: THEME

1. What is the title of the story?

   _____

2. What does Mr. Gutiérrez always say when Pedro asks why he continues to plant corn?

   _____

3. How does Pedro feel about his father's determination to continue planting after the volcano damages their land?

   _____

4. How does Pedro help his family grow a successful crop of corn?

   _____

5. What does Pedro say at the very end of the story?

   _____

6. What do you think is the main message about life that the author wants readers to understand?

   _____

Reading-Writing Connection

What change might you want to make in your life? On a separate sheet of paper, write a paragraph explaining the change. Why might your life be better as a result?

Skill: Reading a Map

BACKGROUND INFORMATION

"Mexico's Natural Resources" is about the rich resources of Mexico, our neighbor to the south. Natural resources are materials supplied by nature. Everything we use from the earth is a natural resource. Soil, water, minerals, plants, and animals are some natural resources. With tools and skills, people can use natural resources to make their lives better.

SKILL FOCUS: Reading a Map

There are many different types of maps. If you have ever taken a long car trip, the driver probably used a road map. Road maps include special symbols to show highways, parks, and highway exits.

Social studies books contain many types of maps. Each type of map shows a different kind of information. Reading the maps along with the text will give you more information.

Three common types of maps are population maps, rainfall maps, and product maps. Each type uses symbols and colors to show special information about a place. The **key** on each map tells what the symbols or colors mean.

Population maps show how many people live in different regions of a country. Colors or symbols on the map show the population density—the average number of people who live in each square mile or square kilometer of a region.

Rainfall maps show the average amount of rain that falls in a region each year. Rainfall is shown in both inches and centimeters. Colors or symbols show the range of rainfall in each region.

Product maps show farm products, minerals, and other natural resources. Picture symbols show the products. The symbols are placed to show which regions produce large amounts of each product.

The following questions will help you read maps.

- Which type of map is this?
- What information does the map show?
- What do the colors or symbols on the map mean?

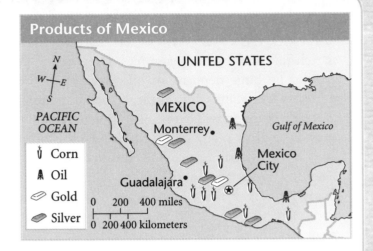

Products of Mexico

▷ Look at the map of Mexico above. What type of map is it? How do you know?

CONTEXT CLUES: Appositive Phrases

An **appositive phrase** explains the meaning of a word that comes just after it. It is often set off by commas or dashes and begins with the word *or*.

Look for the appositive phrase that explains the meaning of fertile in the following sentence.

The soil itself is __fertile__, or rich in minerals that help crops grow.

If you don't know the meaning of *fertile,* just read the words that come after the comma. The appositive phrase *rich in minerals that help crops grow* tells you the meaning of the word.

▷ Read the following sentence. Circle the appositive phrase that explains the meaning of *zinc.*

__Zinc__, a bluish-white mineral, is used to make brass.

As you read the following selection, look for appositive phrases. Use them to find the meaning of the underlined words *staples, arable,* and *irrigation.*

> **Strategy Tip**
>
> As you read, study the maps. They will give you detailed information about Mexico's resources.

Mexico's Natural Resources

MEXICO, OUR NEIGHBOR TO THE SOUTH, is rich in many natural resources. Deep below the ground lie huge deposits of oil, silver, and other minerals. The soil itself is fertile, or rich in minerals that help crops grow. There is also enough rainfall in Mexico to grow many crops. Mexico's thick forests and long coastline provide lumber and fish. Beautiful landscapes and a warm climate attract many tourists. Finally, Mexico has a large, young, and energetic population to make use of all these resources.

Silver and Oil

As early as the 1500s, Mexico's silver attracted Spanish explorers. The Spanish rulers dug many silver mines, and some of these mines still produce silver today. For centuries now, Mexico has been the world's leading silver producer. Most of the silver mines are in central Mexico.

Coal and iron ore are mined in northern Mexico. These natural resources are used in Mexico's steel industry, which is centered around Monterrey (MAHN tə RAY). Mexicans also mine gold, lead, and zinc. Zinc, a bluish-white mineral, is used to make brass.

Oil and natural gas are Mexico's most valuable natural resources. The nation's oilfields are located mainly on the eastern coast around the city of Vera Cruz (VEER ə CROOZ). In the 1980s, large oil deposits were found under the Gulf of Mexico off the nation's eastern coast. Oil-drilling platforms are still pumping this oil from the ocean floor.

Mexico earns much of its income by exporting oil to other countries. When the price of oil rises,

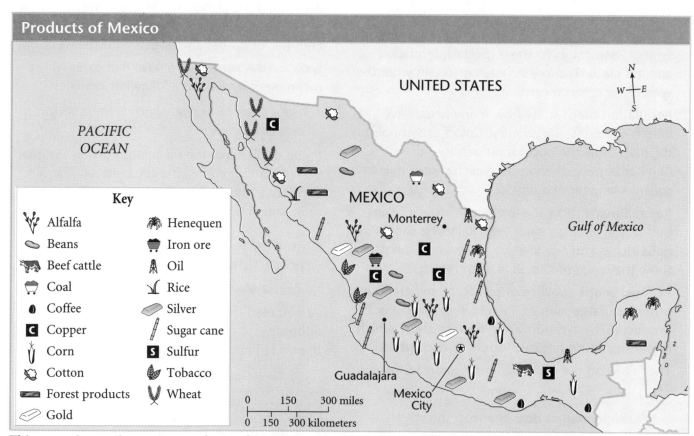

Products of Mexico

PACIFIC OCEAN

UNITED STATES

MEXICO

Monterrey

Gulf of Mexico

Guadalajara

Mexico City

Key

Alfalfa	Henequen
Beans	Iron ore
Beef cattle	Oil
Coal	Rice
Coffee	Silver
Copper	Sugar cane
Corn	Sulfur
Cotton	Tobacco
Forest products	Wheat
Gold	

0   150   300 miles

0   150   300 kilometers

This map shows the major products of Mexico and where they are found.

Mexico's economy benefits. When demand for oil falls, the whole Mexican economy suffers.

Farmlands and Forests

Agriculture has always been one of Mexico's major industries. Before 1917, most farming was done on huge farms controlled by a few rich landowners. Some of these **haciendas** (HAH see EN dəz) had millions of acres. After 1917, the haciendas were broken up. The land was divided among many small farmers. Some small landowners now band together to form shared farms called *ejidos* (ay HEE dohz).

Corn has been the main crop in Mexico for thousands of years. It is usually ground up and baked into flat breads called *tortillas* (tor TEE yəz). This, along with corn, beans, called *frijoles* (free HOH layz), and squash, are the <u>staples</u>, or main foods, of Mexicans.

About one-fifth of Mexico's land is <u>arable</u>, or suitable for crops. The rest is too dry or too mountainous. With <u>irrigation</u>—supplying water with pipes or ditches—cotton and wheat have become major crops in northern Mexico.

Nearly 40 percent of Mexico is pasture land. Pasture land is too dry for crops, but cattle can graze on it. Ranching is especially important in the north. Sheep, goats, pigs, and chickens are raised throughout Mexico.

Forests cover about 20 percent of Mexico. The largest forests are in the mountains of northwestern and central Mexico. There are also forests in the rainy southern and southeastern regions of the country.

Pine trees are logged to make wood pulp and paper. Sapodilla (sahp oh DEE yə) trees in the south provide chicle, which is used to make chewing gum. Mahogany, ebony, and rosewood are some of Mexico's valuable hardwoods. They are used to make furniture.

Over the past 20 years, Mexican forests have been disappearing at a rapid rate. Farming is partly to blame. Farmers have cut down and burned forests to create more farmland. Loggers have also cut

Average Yearly Rainfall in Mexico

PACIFIC OCEAN

Monterrey

Gulf of Mexico

Mexico City

Inches	Centimeters
More than 39	More than 100
20–39	50–100
12–20	30–50
Less than 12	Less than 30

0   200   400 miles
0   200 400 kilometers

This map shows how much rain falls in different parts of Mexico during a year.

Population of Mexico

Tijuana Mexicali

Juarez

Chihuahua

Torreón   Monterrey

Gulf of Mexico

PACIFIC OCEAN

Guadalajara   León   Mérida

Mexico City   Puebla

Persons per square mile	Persons per square kilometer
More than 250	More than 100
60–250	25–100
25–60	10–25
Fewer than 25	Fewer than 10

0   200   400 miles
0   200 400 kilometers

This map shows where the current population of Mexico lives.

many forests. Cutting trees is a source of income for some Mexicans. The loss of the forests, however, may be harmful to both the economy and the environment of Mexico in years to come.

The People of Mexico

Mexico has a fast-growing population. In 1900, there were only 13 million Mexicans. By 2000, the population had grown to more than 100 million people. At present growth rates, Mexico's population will double in less than 30 years.

Three-quarters of all Mexicans live in cities and towns, and many more country people continue to move there. Most of them move in search of jobs. Others come for education or medical care.

The most densely populated part of Mexico is the southern part of the central **plateau** (pla TOH), a flat area high in the mountains. Mexico City, the world's fastest-growing city, is located there. It is the capital of Mexico. Guadalajara (GWAW də lə HAHR ə) is Mexico's second-largest city. It is also on the central plateau, northwest of the capital. Monterrey, the third largest city, is in the northeast, not far from the U.S. border.

Mexico's population is much younger than that of many other countries. Almost 40 percent of its people are under the age of 15. People are also living longer because of the nation's improving medical care. However, the rapidly growing population is causing some social problems for the nation. It is difficult for the government to provide enough social services and jobs for so many people. Providing these services will be a continuing challenge for this rapidly growing nation.

COMPREHENSION

1. What are natural resources?

   _____

   _____

2. How did farming in Mexico change after 1917?

   _____

   _____

3. Explain why country people move to Mexico's cities.

   _____

   _____

4. What is Mexico's most valuable export?

   _____

   _____

5. Where are Mexico's largest forests located?

   _____

   _____

6. How much did Mexico's population grow during the twentieth century?

   _____

   _____

7. Circle the letter of the word that correctly completes the sentence.

   Mexico is the world's leading producer of

   a. silver   **b.** gold   **c.** oil   **d.** zinc

8. Circle the word with the same meaning as the underlined words in each sentence.

   a. Squash is one of the main foods of the Mexican diet.

      luxuries   staples   proteins

   b. Dry, rocky land is not suitable for crops.

      arable   available   affordable

   c. The process of supplying water with pipes or ditches helps Mexicans grow crops in dry areas.

      conservation   sanitation   irrigation

1. Tell why so many of Mexico's people live in and around major cities.

   _____

   _____

2. Explain why farm workers might prefer to work on ejidos rather than haciendas.

   _____

   _____

3. Reread the paragraph with the ✔ next to it. Underline the sentence below that states the paragraph's main idea.

   a. Coal and iron ore are mined in northern Mexico.

   b. Except for silver, Mexico has few major mineral deposits.

   c. Many valuable minerals are mined in Mexico.

   d. Mexico's steel industry uses a great deal of coal and iron ore.

4. When the world's economy is doing well, people all over the whole world use more oil. Describe how this situation might affect Mexico.

   _____

   _____

5. What specific problems might result from the loss of Mexico's forests?

   _____

   _____

6. Mexico is learning to use its natural resources more skillfully each year. Conclude what effect this skillful use of resources might have on the country.

   _____

   _____

SKILL FOCUS: READING A MAP

A. Study the product map of Mexico on page 124. It shows which areas of Mexico produce major products. Use the map and its key to decide whether the following statements are true or false. Write *true* or *false* next to each statement.

   _____ 1. Northwestern and southeastern Mexico both produce forest products.

   _____ 2. There are no farms in northwestern Mexico.

   _____ 3. Oil deposits are found on Mexico's east coast, along the Gulf of Mexico.

_____ 4. Corn, alfalfa, and wheat are some important crops of Mexico.

_____ 5. Both mining and agriculture are centered around Mexico City.

_____ 6. Coffee is a product grown only on Mexico's west coast.

B. A rainfall map of Mexico appears on page 125. It shows the average amount of rain that falls in different parts of Mexico each year. Use the map and its key to decide whether the following statements are true or false. Write *true* or *false* next to each statement.

_____ 1. Some parts of Mexico get fewer than 12 inches (30 centimeters) of rain a year.

_____ 2. In general, northern Mexico gets more rainfall than southern Mexico.

_____ 3. Much of southern Mexico gets more than 39 inches (100 centimeters) of rain per year.

_____ 4. Central Mexico receives some of the heaviest rain in the entire country.

_____ 5. The driest land in Mexico is in the north.

_____ 6. Monterrey receives between 12 and 20 inches (30–50 centimeters) of rain per year.

C. The population map on page 125 shows where most Mexicans live. The cities on the map are the nation's largest cities. Use the map and its key to decide whether the following statements are true or false. Write *true* or *false* next to each statement.

_____ 1. The northwest is the most densely populated part of Mexico.

_____ 2. The central part of Mexico is thinly populated.

_____ 3. More Mexicans live along the seacoast than inland.

_____ 4. The population is most dense in and around Mexico City.

_____ 5. Many areas in northern Mexico have fewer than 25 persons per square mile.

_____ 6. The area around Mexico City has 25 to 60 people per square mile.

Reading-Writing Connection

Find out about the major products of your state. Think of symbols to show them. On a separate sheet of paper, draw a product map of your state. Include a key that tells what each symbol means.

Skill: Reading a Diagram

BACKGROUND INFORMATION

In the selection "Volcanoes," you will learn how and why volcanoes form. Volcanoes have always fascinated, yet terrified, people. It is easy to see why. Volcanoes have caused some of history's worst disasters. The word *volcano* comes from Roman mythology. Ancient Romans believed that Vulcan, the Roman god of fire, lived beneath an island off the coast of Italy. The name of his island was Volcano.

SKILL FOCUS: Reading a Diagram

Diagrams show readers what the words in a text explain. A **diagram** is a drawing that shows the arrangement of things and the relationship of things to each other. When reading a selection with diagrams, read the paragraphs near each diagram first. Then study each diagram. Sometimes a paragraph will include a reference to a diagram, such as "See Figure 1." That is usually the best point to pause in your reading and study the diagram.

When studying a diagram, read the title, the caption, and the labels. The title and the caption tell what the diagram is about. Labels name the parts of the objects shown in the diagram. Sometimes it is helpful to reread the paragraphs that refer to the diagram. By using the diagram and the paragraphs together, you can get a better understanding of what you read.

Use these steps to learn more from diagrams.

1. Read the paragraphs that come just before and just after a diagram. Then study the diagram.

2. As you continue to read, look back at the diagram to get a clearer understanding.

3. Use the diagram and text together to sum up in your own words what you have read.

▶ Study the diagram in the next column. It shows the earth's layers that lie deep beneath a volcano. Then answer the question.

How far below the earth's surface does most magma form?

_____

Layers of Earth Beneath a Volcano

Layers of earth lie deep beneath a volcano.

CONTEXT CLUES: Synonyms

Synonyms are words with the same or similar meanings. Look for synonyms of new or difficult words in the same sentence or in nearby sentences. Synonyms can help you figure out new meanings.

In the following sentences, look for a synonym for the word *molten*.

> The earth is so hot that some of the rock is melted. This **molten** rock often contains gases.

You can figure out the meaning of *molten* from its synonym, *melted*, in the first sentence.

▶ Read the sentence and circle the synonym of the underlined word.

> The long passageway through which lava flows is called a **conduit**.

As you read "Volcanoes," use synonym context clues to understand the meaning of the underlined words *jagged*, *catastrophe*, and *destructive*.

> ### Strategy Tip
> Before you read, study the diagrams, captions and labels to become familiar with the scientific terms.

VOLCANOES

A VOLCANO IS A MOUNTAIN from which hot liquid rock, solid rocks, gases, and ashes are thrown from deep below the earth's surface. This outpouring is called an **eruption** (i RUP shən). Powerful forces below the earth's surface cause volcanic eruptions.

Scientists have theories that explain the eruption of volcanoes. Temperatures deep below the earth's surface are very high. The earth is so hot that some of the rock is melted. This molten rock often contains gases. Molten, or melted, rock is called **magma** (MAG mə).

Magma is lighter than solid rock because it is liquid. Because it is lighter, it slowly rises from deep below the surface and forms a pocket near the surface. This pocket is called a magma chamber.

The magma is under great pressure. It will move from the magma chamber through any broken or weakened part of the solid rock above it. A volcanic eruption occurs when the magma is forced to the earth's surface. When the magma reaches the surface, it blasts or flows out of an opening. Magma that reaches the surface is called **lava** (LAHV ə).

Types of Lava

One type of lava is thick and contains very little water. During an eruption, this lava often dries and hardens as it reaches the earth's surface. If the lava plugs up the openings in the volcano, then no more lava and gases can escape. Pressure builds up again, causing another eruption. This type of lava usually erupts violently. The thick lava flows slowly and cools into rough, jagged sheets of rock. The edges of these sheets are uneven.

Another type of lava is thin and contains a great deal of water. It flows rapidly down a volcano's slopes. The thin lava usually erupts quietly and spreads over a large area. It hardens into smooth, folded sheets of rock.

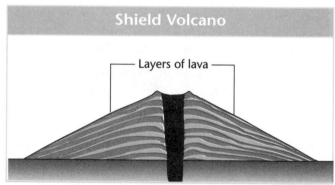

FIGURE 1B.

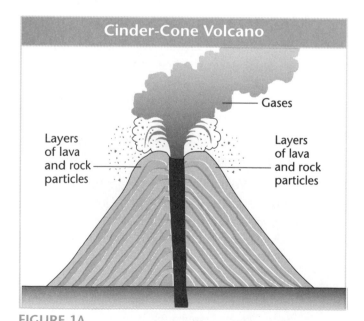

FIGURE 1A.

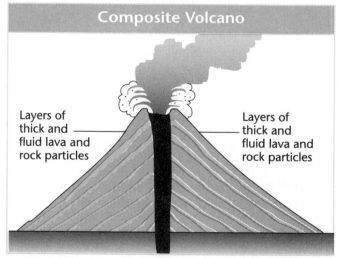

FIGURE 1C.

The shape of a volcano depends on how the volcano was formed.

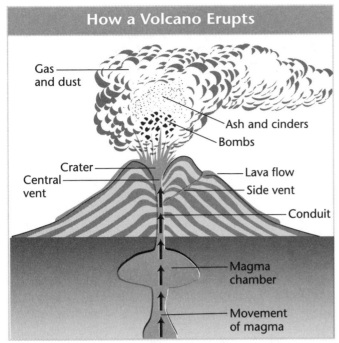

How a Volcano Erupts

Gas and dust

Ash and cinders

Bombs

Crater

Central vent

Lava flow

Side vent

Conduit

Magma chamber

Movement of magma

FIGURE 2. This diagram shows the parts of a volcano through which magma and lava flow.

Types of Volcanoes

Volcanoes are formed by lava eruptions. The **cinder-cone volcano** is formed by violent eruptions of thick lava. Explosions blow lava, gases, and pieces of rock through an opening in the earth. This type of volcano is cone-shaped and has steep sides.

A **shield volcano** is formed by quiet eruptions of thin, quickly flowing lava. The lava flow usually spreads over a low, wide area. Shield volcanoes have gently sloping sides.

A **composite** (kəm poz it) **volcano** is created by eruptions of both thick and thin lava. First a violent eruption occurs. Thick lava bursts out of the earth. This lava hardens, and the ground is covered with pieces of rock. Then a quiet eruption occurs. Thin, flowing lava covers the rocks. The two different types of eruptions continue and build up a composite volcano.

Parts of a Volcano

The long passageway through which lava flows is called a **conduit** (kahn doo ət). The conduit runs from the magma chamber to the opening at the top of the volcano. The opening from which the lava erupts is called the **vent**. Volcanoes often have more than one vent. Cinder-cone volcanoes have a steep-sided pit at the top. This pit is called the **crater**. You can trace the flow of magma and lava through a volcano by studying Figure 2.

Volcanic Rocks

During violent eruptions, pieces of hardened lava, or volcanic rock, are blown into the air. The smallest pieces are called volcanic dust. Slightly larger pieces are called volcanic ash. The largest

SCIENCE

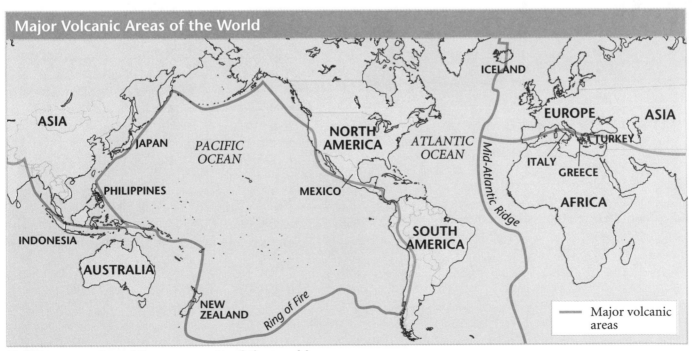

Major Volcanic Areas of the World

ICELAND

ASIA

JAPAN

PACIFIC OCEAN

NORTH AMERICA

ATLANTIC OCEAN

Mid-Atlantic Ridge

EUROPE

ASIA

TURKEY

ITALY

GREECE

PHILIPPINES

MEXICO

AFRICA

INDONESIA

SOUTH AMERICA

AUSTRALIA

NEW ZEALAND

Ring of Fire

— Major volcanic areas

Volcanoes are found in many parts of the world.

pieces of volcanic rock are called cinders or volcanic bombs. Volcanic bombs can weigh several tons.

Where Volcanoes Occur

✔ One of the main areas where volcanoes occur extends all around the edge of the Pacific Ocean. This area is called the Ring of Fire. The ring includes New Zealand, the Philippines, Japan, and the west coasts of North and South America. Volcanoes also occur along the coast of the Mediterranean Sea, between Europe and Africa. Italy, Greece, and Turkey are three countries in that area that have volcanoes. The Mid-Atlantic Ridge is another area where volcanoes occur. This ridge extends from Iceland down the middle of the Atlantic Ocean. You can locate the three areas where volcanoes occur by studying Figure 2.

In these parts of the world, people have always feared volcanoes. Eruptions have occurred throughout history. In A.D. 79, Mount Vesuvius in Italy erupted. This catastrophe destroyed several towns, including Pompeii. The disaster buried Pompeii under more than 12 feet (4 meters) of ashes and cinder. In 1883, Krakatoa, a volcano in Indonesia, erupted violently. The explosion was so loud that people heard it 4,800 kilometers (2,880 miles) away. It caused huge waves in the surrounding ocean. In 1943, a volcano erupted in Mexico. It buried Parícutin and other nearby villages. In 1980, Mount St. Helens erupted in Washington state. Volcanoes are one of the most powerful and destructive forces of nature. Even modern science has found no way to control their harmful effects.

COMPREHENSION

1. What is a volcanic eruption?

   _____

   _____

2. What is magma?

   _____

   _____

3. What is lava?

   _____

   _____

4. What are two types of lava?

   _____

   _____

5. Identify three types of volcanoes.

   _____

   _____

6. What is the crater of a volcano?

   _____

   _____

7. In your own words, explain what happens during the eruption of a volcano. Be sure to use the names of the parts of the volcano.

   _____

   _____

   _____

8. Look at the map on page 131. Explain what the label *Ring of Fire* means.

   _____

   _____

9. Draw a line to match each word with its meaning.

   jagged   a. harmful

   catastrophe   b. uneven

   destructive   c. disaster

In items 1–3, fill in the circle next to the correct answer.

1. The temperature deep inside the earth's surface
   - ○ **a.** is always cold.
   - ○ **b.** is always hot.
   - ○ **c.** is sometimes hot and sometimes cool.
   - ○ **d.** is always cool.

2. Volcanoes occur in areas of the world where
   - ○ **a.** the weather is always very hot.
   - ○ **b.** there is very little water.
   - ○ **c.** there is a great change in weather.
   - ○ **d.** there is shifting of rock under the ground.

3. The paragraph with a ✔ next to it does not have a sentence that directly states the main idea. Choose the sentence below that states this main idea.
   - ○ **a.** Volcanoes can be found in the tropical regions of South America.
   - ○ **b.** Volcanoes are more common in the Southern Hemisphere.
   - ○ **c.** Volcanoes are mainly found in three areas of the world.
   - ○ **d.** Volcanoes are more common in the Northern Hemisphere.

4. Explain why people living in areas where volcanoes erupt have always feared volcanoes.

   _____

   _____

   _____

   _____

SKILL FOCUS: READING A DIAGRAM

Study Figure 2 on page 131. Then write the answers on the lines.

1. In your own words, explain what is happening.

   _____

   _____

2. What is the name of the long passageway through which the lava flows to the surface?

   _____

   _____

3. What is the name of the pocket where the lava pools near the earth's surface?

   _____

   _____

4. What are the names of the openings from which the lava flows?

   _____

   _____

Reading-Writing Connection

What can local governments do to help people living near volcanoes prepare for an eruption? On a separate sheet of paper, write a list of three suggestions.

Skill: Reading Mathematical Terms

BACKGROUND INFORMATION

In "Mathematical Terms for Geometry," you will learn some math terms that will help you when you study geometry. In geometry, you will learn about the shapes and sizes of geometric figures, such as triangles, rectangles, and circles. It is important to understand geometry because our world is filled with geometric shapes. The walls of a room, for example, are usually rectangles. Wheels are circles. The study of geometry begins with understanding points, lines, and angles.

SKILL FOCUS:

Reading Mathematical Terms

We all use words like *line*, *ray*, *angle*, and *point* in everyday life. A line, for example, is a group of people waiting to do something. A ray might be a flash of light or sunshine, an *angle* is a corner of a room, and a point is a main idea.

In mathematics, everyday words have special meanings. To understand geometry, you will need to learn these special meanings. In math, a **line** goes on forever; it never ends. A **ray** is part of a line; it has only one endpoint. An **angle** is formed when two rays meet. A **point** is a position that has no dimensions; it cannot be seen.

The diagrams in your math textbooks will show you what these terms mean. The diagrams, together with the text, will also show you what symbol represents each of the mathematical terms. Study the diagrams carefully as you read. They will help you understand the meanings of mathematical terms and symbols.

▶ Complete each sentence below with the correct mathematical terms.

In mathematics, a _____ is a position with no dimensions.

A _____ goes on forever in two directions.

A _____ has one endpoint, but goes on forever in the other direction.

The word _____ refers to the figure formed when two rays meet.

WORD CLUES

As you read the selection, look for the words *point*, *line*, *line segment*, *endpoints*, *ray*, *angle*, and *vertex*. The diagrams should help you understand these words when they are used in mathematics.

Strategy Tip

When reading "Mathematical Terms for Geometry," pay close attention to the symbols that stand for mathematical terms in the selection. Keep in mind that these symbols are shortened ways of writing mathematical terms.

Mathematical Terms for Geometry

The study of geometry begins with the word **point**. A point has no size. It has neither length nor width. It is usually shown by a dot. The point is named using a capital letter. This is how point S is written.

S

Many, many points that go on forever can be placed next to each other. This is called a **line**. A line has length but no width. A line extends on and on in both directions. It never ends. Arrows on a line show that it never ends. A line can be named using any two points on the line. This is line *ST*. It is written $\overleftrightarrow{ST}$.

A line can also be named using a small letter. This is line *k*. It is written *line k*.

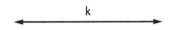

One part of a line is called a **line segment**. A line segment has a beginning and an end. This is line segment *ST*. The points *S* and *T* are fixed. These are called **endpoints**. The symbol for line segment *ST* is $\overline{ST}$. The symbol above the letters has no arrows. This tells you that *ST* is part of a line and has two endpoints.

Another part of a line is called a **ray**. A ray starts at one point and extends on and on in one direction. A ray is named by using two points. The endpoint comes first, followed by a point near the tip of the arrow. The symbol for ray *ST* is $\overrightarrow{ST}$.

This is ray *TS*. The symbol for ray *TS* is $\overrightarrow{TS}$.

When two rays have the same endpoint, they form an **angle**. This is an angle formed by rays *SR* and *ST*.

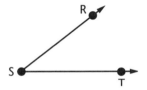

An angle has a **vertex**. The vertex is the common endpoint of the two rays. Point *S* is the vertex of the angle above. The angle also has sides. The sides are the two rays that form the angle. The sides of the angle are $\overrightarrow{ST}$ and $\overrightarrow{SR}$. An angle is named and written using the three points and the symbol for an angle: $\angle RST$ or $\angle TSR$. The point of the vertex is always named in the middle. An angle can also be named using just the point of the vertex: $\angle S$. The angle above can be named $\angle RST$, $\angle TSR$, or $\angle S$.

COMPREHENSION

Fill in the blank to complete each sentence.

1. A _____ has no length or width.

2. Many points going on and on forever form a _____.

3. A part of a line with two endpoints is a _____.

4. Two rays that have a common endpoint form an _____.

5. The common endpoint of two rays that form an angle is called a _____.

6. The rays of an angle are its _____.

1. Explain why this ray is named *AB* and not *BA*.

_____

_____

2. Explain why you can't name angle *XCY* angle *C*.

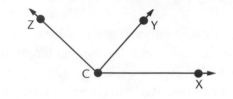

_____

_____

SKILL FOCUS: READING MATHEMATICAL TERMS

A. Below is a map of part of downtown Mexico City. Notice that when roads meet, they form angles. The streets and avenues form rays and line segments. The locations of some buildings look like points.

1. Which building is located at each of these points?

   Point A _____   Point B _____

   Point C _____   Point G _____

2. Which roads are along these rays and line segments?

   $\overrightarrow{AB}$ _____ $\overline{EF}$ _____

   $\overline{CD}$ _____ $\overrightarrow{HG}$ _____

3. Which roads are along these angles?

   ∠GHJ _____

   ∠CDH _____

B. Now practice drawing and naming points, lines, and angles. Use the proper symbols to name line segments, rays, and angles.

1. Draw and label four points.

2. Name three line segments on this line.

_____

_____

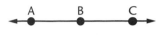

3. Draw line segments connecting points *A*, *B*, *C*, and *D*.

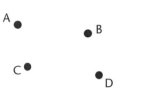

How many line segments can you draw? _____

Name each line segment.

_____

4. Draw and name two rays.

_____

5. Draw two rays with a common endpoint.

6. Draw an angle. Name it three different ways.

_____

7. Name the sides of this angle.

_____

8. Name the vertex of the angle in question 7.

_____

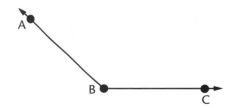

Reading–Writing Connection

An angle is formed when two lines meet. On a separate sheet of paper, write a paragraph describing three angles in your classroom.

Skill: Main Idea and Supporting Details

In reading for details, the first step is to find the **main idea** of the paragraph. The second step is to find the **supporting details** that give more information about the main idea.

The following paragraph is about Christopher Columbus. The main idea and supporting details are listed after the paragraph. Read them.

> Columbus thought that he had reached India when he landed in this part of the world. When he left Spain, his purpose was to find a westward water route for ships sailing to India. When he saw land after ten weeks of sailing, he thought he had found the sought-after water route. He gave the name *Indians* to the people he met on the islands he visited. It was not until some time later that Columbus realized he had not landed on the shores of India.

Main Idea

Columbus thought that he had reached India when he landed in this part of the world.

Supporting Details

a. Columbus wanted to find a water route to India when he sailed from Spain.

b. When Columbus saw land after sailing for a long time, he thought that he had reached India.

c. He called the people Indians.

d. Later Columbus realized that he had not found India.

For each paragraph below, write the sentence that states the main idea. Then, write the major supporting details in your own words. Complete your work on page 139.

> 1. American Indians, or Native Americans, lived in different kinds of houses. American Indians who lived near the Great Lakes used wigwams. Those groups that lived on the Great Plains used tipis. In Eastern Woodland areas, several families lived together in longhouses. In the Southwest, families lived in houses made of adobe brick.
>
> 2. American Indians also traveled in a variety of ways, depending on where they lived. Those who lived near water made boats of reed, which were very light, and canoes. Some canoes were made out of tree bark and were easy to carry. Other canoes, called dugouts, were carved from tree trunks and carried as many as 60 people. American Indians who did not live near water traveled on foot for centuries. After the Spanish introduced horses to North America in the 1600s, American Indians in the Great Plains traveled on horseback.
>
> 3. The daily diet of American Indians came from the crops they grew and the animals they hunted. For example, the groups of American Indians that lived on the Great Plains hunted wild animals, such as buffalo and elk, for food. The Pueblos raised corn, beans, and squash. Groups in the Southeast gathered wild nuts and fruits, hunted deer, and planted crops. Many groups also caught fish in nearby streams.
>
> 4. The American Indians made many things they needed. They made hatchets from stone. Their arrowheads were made of flint, and their bows were made of wood. They made their garments out of deer, elk, or caribou skin. Many also used clay to make pottery.

Paragraph 1:
Main Idea: _____

Supporting Details:

   a. _____

   b. _____

   c. _____

   d. _____

Paragraph 2:
Main Idea: _____

Supporting Details:

   a. _____

   b. _____

   c. _____

Paragraph 3:
Main Idea: _____

Supporting Details:

   a. _____

   b. _____

   c. _____

   d. _____

Paragraph 4:
Main Idea: _____

Supporting Details:

   a. _____

   b. _____

   c. _____

   d. _____

Skill: Outlining

Making an outline is one way to help you remember what you read. An **outline** is a listing of the important ideas, or main ideas, from a selection. A good outline shows how the main ideas and supporting details in a selection are organized and related.

The main ideas in a selection are written next to Roman numerals: I, II, III, IV, V, and so on. The supporting details that give more information about each of the main ideas are written next to capital letters: A, B, C, D, E, and so on. This is called a **two-step outline.** The Roman numerals and capital letters are arranged so that you can easily see the information.

The following is a paragraph about American Indians and an outline of the paragraph. Illustrations are included.

American Indians lived in different kinds of houses. Those who lived in the Great Lakes region used wigwams. Those who lived on the Great Plains used tipis. In the Eastern Woodlands region, several families lived together in longhouses. In the Southwest, American Indians lived in houses made of adobe brick.

American Indians

I. Different kinds of homes

    A. Wigwams—Great Lakes

    B. Tipis—Great Plains

    C. Longhouses—Eastern Woodlands

    D. Adobe brick—Southwest

An outline gives only key words. Each phrase begins with a capital letter. Notice that *Different kinds of homes* is written next to Roman numeral I. These are the key words in the main idea of the paragraph. *Wigwams—Great Lakes* is written next to capital letter A. This phrase gives the key words in the first detail about American Indian homes in the paragraph. The other details are written next to capital letters B, C, and D.

Several other facts are important to know about making an outline. Every outline should have a title. When you outline a selection, remember to include at least two important main ideas from what you have read. An outline of a selection can never have a Roman numeral I without a Roman numeral II. Likewise, at least two supporting details should come under each Roman numeral. An A should always be followed by a B.

Below is more information about American Indians. In Lesson 45, you found the main ideas and supporting details for each paragraph. Now use the two-step outline form to outline the paragraphs. Use the sample outline on page 140 as a model.

American Indians also traveled in variety of ways, depending on where they lived. Those who lived near water made boats of reed, which were very light, and canoes. Some canoes were made out of tree bark and were easy to carry. Other canoes, called dugouts, were carved from tree trunks and carried as many as 60 people. American Indians who did not live near water traveled on foot for centuries. After the Spanish introduced horses to North America in the 1600s, American Indians in the Great Plains traveled on horseback.

The daily diet of American Indians came from the crops they grew and the animals they hunted. For example, the groups of American Indians that lived on the Great Plains killed wild animals, such as buffalo and elk, for food. The Pueblos raised corn, beans, and squash. Groups in the Southeast gathered wild nuts and fruits, hunted deer, and planted crops. Many groups also caught fish in nearby streams.

Competing in athletic games was a favorite pastime of American Indians. Foot racing and different kinds of ballgames were popular in many areas. Usually only women played shinny, a kind of field hockey that was common in North America. Groups of American Indians that lived in the northern regions of North America enjoyed a game called snow snake, in which each player tried to slide a dart or spear the farthest on the snow or ice.

II. _____

    A. _____

    B. _____

    C. _____

III. _____

    A. _____

    B. _____

    C. _____

    D. _____

IV. _____

    A. _____

    B. _____

    C. _____

Skill: Using Guide Words

At the top of each dictionary page are two words in boldface type. These words are called **guide words.** Guide words help you find entry words easily and quickly. They tell you the first and the last entry word on the page. All the other entry words on the page come between these two words in alphabetical order.

Following are some guide words that might appear at the top of some pages in a dictionary.

Page 97:	**bird/bite**		Page 537:	**miracle/misery**
Page 120:	**camp/candle**		Page 653:	**poke/polite**
Page 205:	**clock/cloud**		Page 797:	**slip/slouch**
Page 310:	**figured/filter**		Page 900:	**trade/trap**
Page 403:	**hummock/hurry**		Page 942:	**ward/wary**

Underline all of the words that you would find on the following pages.

1. Page 97

birth   bitter   Bible   biscuit   beach   baboon   bison   bomb

2. Page 120

cane   cacao   cancel   canvas   chain   canal   clay   campus

3. Page 205

crude   clip   clog   camera   comb   court   clot   cactus

4. Page 310

flood   film   fortress   file   finger   faction   filbert   fawn

5. Page 403

hulk   humus   hydra   hoof   hurdle   humid   hygiene   hovel

6. Page 537

minor   Mars   mildew   mirth   motor   middy   mustard   miser

7. Page 653

poise   punt   polar   pliant   policy   portal   prattle   pungent

8. Page 797

slope   screen   slot   slug   sleuth   smug   snipe   slew

9. Page 900

trace   traffic   tragic   track   train   tramp   tropic   trail

10. Page 942

ware   want   warm   wart   wall   warn   wash   warrant

Skill: Using a Dictionary

A **dictionary entry** includes the entry word and all the information about it. The entry word always appears in boldface type. If the word has more than one syllable, it is divided into syllables to show where the word can be divided at the end of a line of writing. The entry word is followed by a **respelling** of the word in parentheses. The respelling shows you how to pronounce the word. The **part-of-speech** label follows the respelling. The labels are usually abbreviated as follows: *adj.* for adjective, *adv.* for adverb, *conj.* for conjunction, *interj.* for interjection, *n.* for noun, *prep.* for preposition, *pron.* for pronoun, and *v.* for verb.

The **definitions** are arranged according to parts of speech. For example, if an entry has noun meanings, all the noun meanings are grouped together and numbered following the label *n.* Any meanings that the word may have for any other part of speech are numbered and placed after the proper label. When an entry has only one meaning for any part of speech, the definition is not numbered. At the end of some entries are phrases or idioms. An **idiom** is a group of words that has a meaning different from the meaning that the individual words have by themselves. In some dictionaries, idioms have a dash in front of them and appear in boldface type.

nose (nōz) *n.* 1 the part of your head that sticks out between the mouth and the eyes and has two openings for breathing and smelling. The nose is part of the muzzle or snout in animals. 2 the sense of smell [a dog with a good *nose*]. 3 the ability to find out things [a reporter with a *nose* for news]. 4 anything like a nose in shape or in the way it is placed, as the front of an airplane or the bow of a ship. ◆ *v.* 1 to move with the front end forward [The ship *nosed* into the harbor]. 2 to meddle in another's affairs. 3 to smell with the nose. 4 to rub with the nose. –**nosed, nos'ing** –**by a nose,** by just a little bit [to win *by a nose*]. –**look down one's nose at,** to be scornful of: used only in everyday speech. –**nose out,** to win by just a little bit. –**on the nose,** exactly; precisely: *a slang phrase* [You guessed the score *on the nose*.] –**pay through the nose,** to pay more than something is worth. –**turn up one's nose at,** to sneer at; to scorn. –**under one's nose,** in plain view.

Use the dictionary entry above to answer the following questions.

1. What is the entry word? _____

2. Write the respelling. _____

3. How many noun meanings follow the part-of-speech label *n.*? _____

4. Write the second verb meaning. _____

5. Write the third noun meaning _____

6. How many idioms are given following the meanings? _____

7. What is the first idiom? _____

8. What is the idiom that you would use only in everyday speech? _____

9. What is the slang idiom that means *exactly*? _____

10. How do you spell the past tense of *nose*? _____

Skill: Reading a Menu

How do you know what to order when you go to a restaurant? The best thing to do is to look at the **menu**. A menu lists all of the different foods that the restaurant serves and gives the price of each item.

The following menu is from a Mexican restaurant, so most of the dishes on the menu have Spanish names. As you read the menu, notice the headings, which identify the types of foods served in the restaurant.

TACO JOE'S RESTAURANT

6116 First Avenue   Open Seven Days a Week

APPETIZERS
NACHOS   melted cheese on tortilla chips with jalapeño pepper   3.50
GUACAMOLE mashed avocados, onions, tomatoes, with
    tortilla chips   3.50
ENSALADA lettice, onions, tomatoes, egg,
    and avocado   (regular) 4.50
    (small) 3.50

SOUPS
SOPA DE POLLO chicken soup   3.25
SOPA DE FRIJOLES NEGROS black bean soup   3.50

ENTRÉES
TACOS   3 crisp-folded corn tortillas* stuffed with ground beef
    or chicken   6.25
ENCHILADAS 3 tortillas stuffed with cheese, beef, or chicken,
    topped with melted cheese and red hot Mexican sauce   6.50
BURRITOS 3 rolled flour tortillas stuffed with chunks of beef   6.50
TOSTADOS 3 open crisp tortillas topped with beans, ground beef,
    and lettuce   6.50
JOE'S COMBINATION chicken taco, cheese enchillada,
    and beef burrito   6.75
POLLO A LA MEXICANA chicken with tomatoes, onions,
    and green peppers   8.25

*a very thin, round pancake

STEAK RANCHERO sliced steak with tomatoes, onions,
    and peppers   8.75
CAMARONES VERACRUZANA shrimp with tomatoes and
    peppers in a deep-fried flour shell   10.25

SIDE ORDERS
Refried beans topped with cheese   3.00
Vegetable of the day   2.50
Basket of tortilla chips   2.25

DESSERTS
FLAN   caramel custard   3.50
MANGO   tropical fruit topped with whipped cream   4.25
ICE CREAM vanilla or chocolate   2.00
NATILLA   Spanish cream and pudding   2.50

BEVERAGES
Coffee   1.00
Tea   1.00
Milk   .85
Juice   .85

A. Use the information on the menu to answer the questions below and on page 145.

1. Which three entrées cost the same? _____

2. What is the most expensive entrée on the menu? _____

3. Which three different stuffings can you order in enchiladas? _____

4. Which two entrées can you choose between if you want to eat both chicken and cheese?

    _____

5. Which dessert is a kind of fruit? _____

6. If you do not want to eat onions, which appetizer must you choose? _____

7. Why won't a vegetarian order Joe's Combination?

   _____

8. How are the tortillas used for tacos different from those used for burritos?

   _____

9. How are the tortillas used for tacos similar to those used for tostados? _____

10. You have $9.25 to spend on dinner. You have already ordered tacos and milk. Which

    dessert can you afford? _____

11. Figure the cost of the following meals.

guacamole	$ _____	sopa de pollo	$ _____	small ensalada	$ _____
sopa de frijoles negros	_____	steak ranchero	_____	beef enchiladas	_____
tacos	_____	broccoli	_____	beans with cheese	_____
tea	_____	juice	_____	flan	_____
Total	$ _____	Total	$ _____	Total	$ _____

12. Find the least expensive meal in question 11. List the menu heading for each item in that meal.

    _____

B. **Read each statement about the menu, and decide whether the statement is true or false. Then write *true* or *false* on each line.**

_____ 1. Flan is a kind of Spanish soup.

_____ 2. Ensalada is a salad.

_____ 3. The ingredients in guacamole include avocados, onions, and tomatoes.

_____ 4. You can order a cheeseburger and French fries at Taco Joe's restaurant.

_____ 5. Six of the entrées are prepared with tortillas.

_____ 6. Taco Joe's is closed on Sundays.

_____ 7. By reading the menu, you can learn that the Spanish word for chicken is *pollo*.

_____ 8. If you have $10.00 to spend at Taco Joe's, you have enough money to order burritos, a
            vegetable, and a mango.

_____ 9. If you have $10.00 to spend at Taco Joe's, you have enough money to order pollo a la
            Mexicana and milk.

_____ 10. Natilla is served with rice and beans.

Neighbors to the South

LESSON 50

Skill: Plot

BACKGROUND INFORMATION

"The Giant Snake That Swallowed a Girl" is a folk tale from Colombia, a country in South America. A folk tale has no known author. Most folk tales have been passed down by word of mouth for centuries before they were written down. Unlike myths, which tell about gods and heroes, folk tales have ordinary people for characters.

SKILL FOCUS: Plot

A **plot** is a series of events that make up a story. The plot is "what happens" in the story. The plots of most stories follow the pattern shown in this diagram.

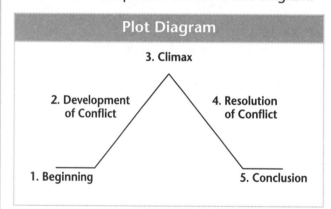

Plot Diagram

3. Climax

2. Development of Conflict

4. Resolution of Conflict

1. Beginning

5. Conclusion

1. **Beginning**   The events at the beginning of a story introduce the characters and the setting and make you interested in what will happen.

2. **Conflict**   Soon a conflict develops. It might be a conflict between two characters or a conflict between a character and an outside force.

3. **Climax**   The plot events gradually build to the climax. This is the part when you are most excited or worried about what will happen next.

4. **Resolution**   The events that follow the climax resolve the main conflict in the story. This part of the story is called the resolution.

5. **Conclusion**   A conclusion, or final event, then ends the story.

▶ Think of a story you have read or a movie you have seen. Does the plot follow the basic pattern shown in the diagram? Copy the Plot Diagram on this page onto a separate sheet of paper. Fill in the appropriate events under each label.

CONTEXT CLUES: Using a Dictionary

When you read a new word, context clues may give you a general idea of its meaning. However, you may need more details to really understand the word. If so, look up the word in a **dictionary**.

Read the following sentence and think about the meaning of the underlined word.

To his horror, he saw an __anaconda__, the longest snake in the jungle.

The context clues tell you that an anaconda is a long snake. To know more about this snake, look up *anaconda* in a dictionary. You will learn that an anaconda can grow to 30 feet long. It is related to a boa constrictor. It squeezes its prey with coils and swallows its prey whole.

▶ Look up the meaning of the underlined word in the sentence below. Write its definition on the lines.

An anaconda can swallow a goat or a __peccary__.

_____

_____

As you read, use a dictionary to find out more about the meanings of *serpent*, *paca*, and *mammoths*.

Strategy Tip

As you read, use the Plot Diagram on this page to keep track of the events in the story.

The Giant Snake That Swallowed a Girl

Long, long ago, a South American Indian named Magu spent the night far out in the jungle of the land now known as Colombia. He made himself a soft bed of leaves on the bank of a stream. He slept soundly.

When he awoke in the morning, he felt something move against his side. To his horror, he saw an anaconda, the longest snake in the jungle. Magu could see its spots clearly as it crawled away and slipped into the river.

"I have had a narrow escape," Magu said to himself. "Although the anaconda does not bite, its strong coils could easily have crushed me while I slept."

Magu stood up, and he looked all around to make sure that no other <u>serpent</u> was near. In his search, he discovered that the giant snake had left an egg in the leaves. It was a soft, leathery egg, almost as big as a gourd.

"Ho, this will amuse my wife and my daughter, Mina." Magu picked up the egg and carried it home.

There he told his strange tale. When his wife and child had examined the egg, they laid it on a warm ledge near the cooking fire. They forgot it until 14 days had gone by. Then the egg's covering broke, and a young anaconda crawled out.

"Kill the snake! Kill it, my husband!" Magu's wife, Malani, cried.

"No," said Magu. "Why should we kill such a pretty, young creature? See its handsome markings! Look how big it is! An anaconda has no teeth and no poison. I shall keep it for a pet."

"Ah, but an anaconda can squeeze, Magu," Malani objected. "An anaconda can swallow a goat

or a peccary. I do not like having a giant snake live in our hut."

"I will give my snake animals out of my traps in the jungle. I will feed it fish from the river. I will keep its stomach filled at all times. Then it will be content. It will harm no one," said Magu.

Curiously, Magu was able to tame the anaconda quickly. It lived happily inside his hut. The man brought it plenty of his small animals and fish, which it greatly liked. When Magu called, "Boya! Boya!" the snake would crawl out of its corner and swallow its meal in one mighty gulp. It ate and ate. It grew and it grew. It was truly much bigger than any other anaconda in the jungle.

Magu's pet snake was so long that it would reach from the ridge of the roof to the ground. Its body was thicker than a man's thigh. Amazingly, though, it was tame, just as tame as Mina's pet parrot.

The snake seemed to love its master. Sometimes it followed him into the forest and looped itself around a tree branch nearby while Magu fished or shot turtles with his flying arrows. Always it came back with him to the hut at night.

Magu's wife and daughter did not like the serpent. Malani shook her head and said over and over, "This is not good, my husband. One day you will be sorry." Little Mina was afraid of the giant snake.

Now Magu loved his small daughter, Mina, more than anything else in the world. Unfortunately, the tame anaconda was jealous of her. Whenever the man played with Mina, the brown snake would coil itself up in a corner and sulk. It would not come out again until Magu had called it and called it. Yet the strange pet never tried to do the child harm.

One day, a feast was to be held in a neighboring village. For weeks, Magu's family had thought about the eating and talking, the singing and dancing that there would be.

As bad luck would have it, Mina fell ill a short time before the feast. Though she was almost well enough on the day of the feast, she did not want to go.

"I shall not be lonely while you are gone, Papita, Mamita. I shall have Papagayo here to talk to." She held her finger out to her parrot, which she loved well. She begged her parents to go. They went off down the river in their canoe.

All would have been well if Magu had not forgotten to feed his snake that day. That day the giant snake was hungry. It crawled out of its dark corner, looking for food. Possibly it was hunger. Perhaps it was jealousy of Mina, who took up so much of the master's attention. Whatever the reason, the giant jaws opened wide. With one mighty gulp, the anaconda swallowed the girl.

Papagayo, the parrot, screamed when it saw what had taken place. It flapped its wings wildly and darted out of the hut door. Across the forest to the neighboring village it flew. There it circled among the merrymakers until it found Magu.

In those times, parrots could say many, many more words than such birds today, which only repeat what they have been taught.

"Master! Master!" the parrot squawked into the ear of the surprised Magu. "Master, come quickly! The snake has eaten poor Mina! It has swallowed her whole!"

Magu lost no time in getting back to his hut. Beside the cooking fire, he found the anaconda asleep. Magu could see his child's slim form under the scaly skin of the big snake. Having no teeth, anacondas swallow their food whole. When their stomachs are full, they straightaway go to sleep.

"Boya! Boya!" The father shouted the name by which he called his pet. "Wake, Boya! Give me back my daughter!"

Once more the man called while the parrot screamed. However, the snake would not wake up.

Then Magu made a plan. He brought in a freshly killed paca from his traps and laid it on the ground close to the snake. He then heated a small stone until it was red hot and put it down nearby.

The smell of the freshly killed paca, which the snake liked so well, made the sluggish creature lift up its head and open its eyes. The greedy serpent spread its jaws wide to swallow the paca. At that moment, Magu threw the hot stone far down its open throat.

How the snake choked and coughed! It opened its burned throat so wide that it brought up the stone, and with it Magu's daughter. When her father picked her up off the ground, Mina was unhurt.

What became of the giant snake Boya? Magu did not risk his child's life a second time. He told the anaconda to go away and never come back. No doubt the scar left in the snake's throat reminded it that Magu would have no pity on it if it did.

Travelers still tell fabulous tales about the giant snakes, like Magu's Boya, that live in the jungles along the equator. Some say that these serpents are not really long enough to swallow a child. Others remind them that this story happened long, long ago. Perhaps it happened in prehistoric times when mammoths and giant snakes may have lived on the Earth.

The South American Indians of this part of Colombia say that the winding streams of their homeland are the tracks left by such enormous serpents. They say that when a lake dries up, its serpent has gone away and will not come back again.

COMPREHENSION

1. When and where does this story take place?

_____

_____

2. What happens to the egg after Magu carries it home?

_____

_____

3. How do Magu and his wife feel about keeping the snake after it hatches?

_____

_____

4. Describe Boya, Magu's pet anaconda.

_____

_____

5. Why does Mina stay home from the feast in a neighboring village?

_____

_____

6. Which does Mina prefer to have as a pet—Boya the snake or Papagayo the parrot?

_____

_____

7. Give two possible reasons for Boya's swallowing Mina.

_____

_____

8. a. Why does Magu bring a freshly killed paca near the snake when he gets home?

_____

_____

b. How does Magu save his daughter?

_____

_____

9. Draw a line from each word to its correct meaning.

serpent   a. extinct hairy elephants

mammoths   b. tailless rodent

paca   c. snake

CRITICAL THINKING

1. Discuss why Magu is unwise for keeping the giant anaconda for a pet.

_____

_____

_____

2. Explain why the egg was able to hatch in the hut.

_____

_____

_____

3. Discuss what you think Magu learns from his experience.

_____

_____

_____

4. Predict what you think happens to the giant anaconda after it leaves.

_____

_____

_____

5. Do you think that the events in the story really happened? Explain.

_____

_____

_____

Below is a list of events from the story. Starting where it says *Beginning,* fill in the events in the correct parts of the diagram below. If necessary, review the Skill Focus on page 146 before you begin.

Magu decides to keep as a pet the anaconda that hatched from an egg he brought home.

Magu tells Boya to go away and never return.

The snake swallows Mina.

The snake, although tame and fond of Magu, grows jealous of Mina.

Magu uses a paca and a hot stone to trick Boya into coughing up his daughter.

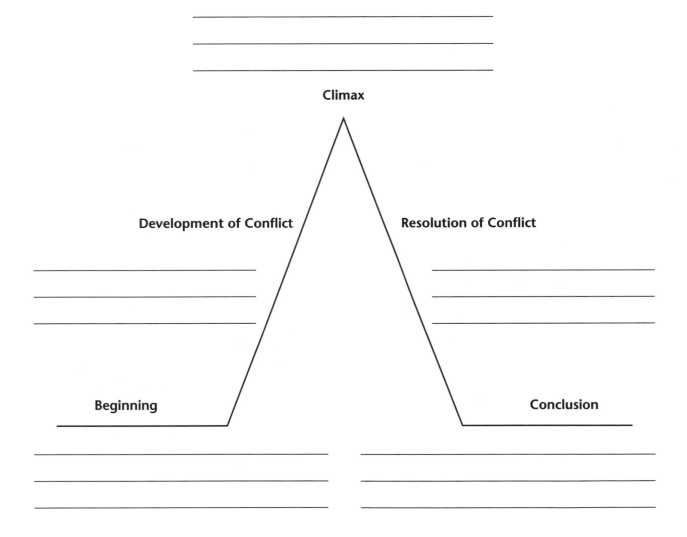

Climax

Development of Conflict

Resolution of Conflict

Beginning

Conclusion

Reading-Writing Connection

Do you know another folk tale that teaches a lesson? On a separate sheet of paper, write the folk tale in your own words.

Skill: Comparing and Contrasting

BACKGROUND INFORMATION

In "The Humid Subtropics", you will read about two regions of the Western Hemisphere known as the humid subtropics. The climate there affects how the people live. Climate is the average weather in an area over a long period of time. Average temperatures and average rainfall determine the climate of a region. The average temperature of a region is determined mainly by its distance north or south of the equator. The closer a region is to the equator, the warmer it is.

SKILL FOCUS: Comparing and Contrasting

Noticing how things are alike is **comparing**. Noticing how they are different is **contrasting**. Comparing and contrasting are important ways to understand information.

One way a writer can show comparison and contrast is to describe a key feature of one subject and then describe the same feature of another subject. In this way, a writer shows how the two subjects are alike or different.

The following paragraphs compare and contrast the climates of the Northeastern and Southeastern United States. In the first paragraph, the writer describes the winters in each area. In the second paragraph, the writer describes the summers in each area.

The Northeast has cold, snowy winters. The average January temperature varies from 15° to 30°F. The Southeast, however, has mild winters with little snow. Average January temperatures there range from 40° to over 65°F.

Summers in the Northeast are warm, with July temperatures varying from 60° to 75°F. In contrast, summers in the Southeast are hotter and more humid.

When you read for comparisons and contrasts, also look for signal words and phrases. The words *similar, same, like, also,* and *both* show similarities. The words *unlike, however, but, different,* and *on the contrary* show differences.

Look back at the paragraphs about the climate of the Northeast and the Southeast. Use the details you find to complete this Comparison and Contrast Chart.

Climate of the Northeast and Southeast		
Season	**Northeast**	**Southeast**
winter		
summer		

CONTEXT CLUES: Definitions

Your textbooks often contain **definitions** of new words. You will find these definitions in the sentences before or after the new word.

Find the context clues that define the underlined word in these sentences.

*Major crops are grown in the **Pampas**. The Pampas is the large, fertile, grassy plain of Argentina.*

If you don't know the meaning of *Pampas*, read on to the next sentence. It gives you the definition.

Circle the definition of the word *phosphate* in the following sentences.

*Most of the nation's **phosphate** comes from Florida and Tennessee. Phosphate is a salt used in fertilizer.*

As you read the selection, look for definitions to help you understand the meanings of the underlined words *reserves, tourism,* and *revenue*.

Strategy Tip

As you read "The Humid Subtropics," look for comparisons and contrasts. Use signal words and the way the paragraphs are organized to find similarities and differences.

The Humid Subtropics

THE AREAS OF THE EARTH closest to the equator are called the **tropics** (TRAHP iks). These areas have a hot, steamy climate all year round. Just north and south of the tropics are the **subtropics**. These areas are hot and **humid** (HYOO mid), or damp, in the summer. They have very mild winters. They are often called the humid subtropics.

The humid subtropic regions of the Western Hemisphere lie in the eastern parts of North and South America between latitudes 25 degrees and 38 degrees. In North America, this region is called the U.S. South. It includes the southeastern part of the United States, from the southeastern coast westward to Oklahoma and Texas. In South America, the region is located in the south-central part of the continent. It includes northeastern Argentina, all of Uruguay, most of southern Brazil, and the southern part of Paraguay.

Climate

✗ The humid subtropics have hot, wet summers and mild winters. In the summer, they have high humidity (hyoo MID ə tee). This means that the air is heavy with water vapor. They also have high temperatures, often above 90 degrees Fahrenheit (32 degrees Celsius). Winters are usually mild.

However, it sometimes does snow in the southern United States. The reason for this is simple. The North American continent touches the Arctic region. There are no mountain barriers to block cold Arctic air masses from moving south. The cold air masses often bring cold weather, and sometimes snow, to the southern part of the United States.

In contrast, snow is rare in the South American humid subtropics. This region is separated from the Antarctic region by water. By the time a cold air mass crosses the southern Atlantic Ocean and reaches the continent, the air mass is no longer very cold.

Agriculture

The humid subtropics have plenty of rainfall, warmth, and a long growing season. These are excellent conditions for farming. Farmers can grow a variety of crops, including fruits, vegetables, and grains.

Crops of the U.S. South include cotton, corn, peanuts, tobacco, and soybeans. Fruits are also important crops. These include oranges and grapefruits in Florida and peaches in the Carolinas and Georgia. Sugar cane grows in the Florida Everglades. Farmers in Louisiana and Texas grow rice. Tobacco is another major crop of this region. Livestock and beef cattle are also important.

The South American humid subtropics also have excellent conditions for farming. Major crops are grown in the Pampas. The Pampas is the large,

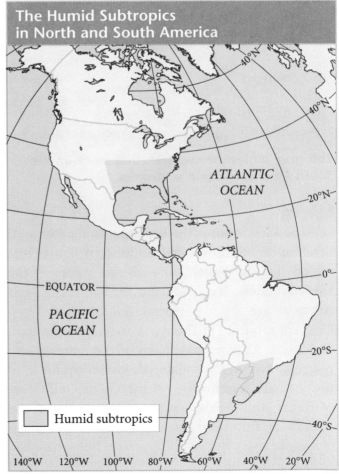

The Humid Subtropics in North and South America

Humid subtropics

The shaded areas show the humid subtropics in North and South America.

SOCIAL STUDIES

fertile, grassy plain of Argentina. Wheat, corn, sunflowers, and flax for seed are the leading crops. Ranchers also grow millions of acres of alfalfa to feed local cattle. In many parts of this region, livestock grazing is more important than farming. Today much of the world's supply of fresh beef comes from this region.

This map shows the countries that make up the South American humid subtropics.

Mining

The U.S. South is the leading mining region of the humid subtropics. In the western half of the region lies the largest oil and gas supply in the United States. Texas, Oklahoma, Louisiana, and Arkansas are the major producers of oil and gas. Coal is found in Oklahoma, Alabama, Mississippi, and Texas. Alabama has much of the nation's iron reserves. Reserves are materials stored up for later use. Bauxite is mined in Arkansas. The Gulf Coast of Texas and Louisiana produces much of the world's sulfur. Most of the nation's phosphate comes from Florida and Tennessee. Phosphate is a salt used in fertilizer.

In contrast, the South American humid subtropic region does not have important mineral deposits. The

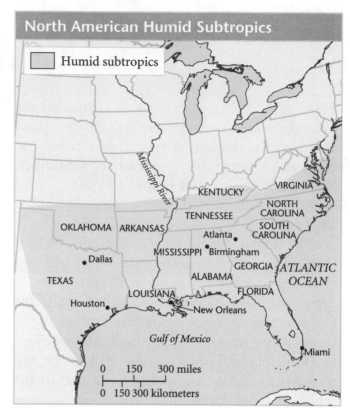

This map shows the areas in the United States that make up the North American humid subtropics.

only important deposits are in Brazil, which has some small coal fields in its southern states.

Manufacturing

✗ Several conditions are necessary for a manufacturing economy. A region needs mines, forests, fields, and the sea to provide raw materials. Coal, oil, natural gas, and water are needed to produce power. Labor and money must be available. Good transportation systems are needed to ship goods to markets.

The U.S. South has all of these conditions. As a result, the economy in this region depends on manufacturing. The textile mills of this region lead the nation in the making of cotton goods. The region is also a leader in the making of rayon. Pulp and paper industries are important. The South also has many hosiery mills, furniture factories, and iron and steel plants.

✔ In contrast, not all of the conditions necessary for manufacturing exist in the South American humid subtropics. As a result, this region produces raw materials that must be processed in other countries. The only important industries are the preparing of wheat and meat for export and the production of textiles for local markets.

Urban Centers

Some of the largest cities of the world are in the humid subtropic regions. The growth of industries there has promoted the development of large cities.

When the U.S. South was mainly a farming region, cities were small and few in number. In the last few decades, however, urban areas have increased in size. The largest cities of the region are Houston, Dallas, Atlanta, New Orleans, Miami, and Birmingham.

Like the North American humid subtropics, the South American humid subtropics include major cities. In contrast, however, the region has fewer urban centers. Three important cities in the region are Buenos Aires, Montevideo, and Rosario.

Buenos Aires has close to 13 million people and is the largest city in Argentina. It is also the capital city. It has a good harbor, rich soil, and land and water transportation. For these reasons, it is Argentina's major port and its center of commerce, industry, and government.

Montevideo, with over 1.3 million people, is the leading city in Uruguay. It is the center of the nation's industry, as well as its capital.

Rosario, Argentina, is the third largest city of the region. It has a population of almost 1 million and is located 200 miles (320 kilometers) north of Buenos Aires.

Tourism

<u>Tourism</u> is an important industry in the humid subtropic regions. Tourism is the business of entertaining, housing, and guiding travelers. It is an important source of <u>revenue</u>. Revenue is the money taken in by businesses and governments.

Each winter, thousands of tourists travel to the U.S. South, especially the coastal areas. Florida has become the recreation center of the region. Each year, its tourism brings in billions of dollars. Mild winter weather, beach resorts, and sport fishing attract many tourists. The region also has many interesting cities and historical sites that draw visitors.

Leading tourist areas in the South American humid subtropics include Buenos Aires and the beaches of Uruguay. Since air travel is so easy, tourists from around the world visit these South American resort areas.

With their warm, wet climates, both the North and South American humid subtropics remain important farming areas. Both areas are now using more of their raw materials and energy resources to develop new industries, too. This growth has resulted in large cities and a booming tourist trade in both regions. Despite their many similarities, however, major differences between the North and South American humid subtropics remain.

This cotton field in Mississippi is one of many scenes in the North American humid subtropics.

1. Where is the North American humid subtropic region located?

   _____

2. Where is the South American humid subtropic region located?

   _____

3. Read the two paragraphs with an ✗ next to them. For each paragraph, underline the sentence that tells the main idea.

4. Why is it too warm for snow in the South American humid subtropics?

   _____

5. Write the letter of the correct meaning next to each word.

   _____ reserves   **a.** the guiding of travelers

   _____ tourism   **b.** money collected by a government

   _____ revenue   **c.** things stored up for later use

CRITICAL THINKING

1. Explain why there are fewer urban centers in the South American humid subtropics than in the North American humid subtropics.

   _____

   _____

   _____

2. Reread the paragraph with a ✔ next to it. Circle the letter of the statement that tells the main idea of the paragraph.

   a. Raw materials can easily be sent to South American markets.

   b. In the South American humid subtropics, manufacturing is relatively unimportant.

   c. In the South American humid subtropics, there are good transportation systems.

   d. All the conditions necessary for manufacturing exist in the South American humid subtropics.

A. Complete the Comparisons Chart below to show the features of the North and South American humid subtropic regions that are alike. Skim each section of the selection to find one important similarity. Then write a sentence describing it. The first one is done for you.

Comparisons	
Feature	**North and South American Humid Subtropics**
climate	Both regions have hot, wet summers and mild winters.
agriculture	
urban centers	
tourism	

B. Use the same procedure to complete the Contrasts Chart below to show the differences. The first one is done for you.

Contrasts		
Feature	**North American Humid Subtropics**	**South American Humid Subtropics**
climate	This region has snow because cold Arctic air can reach it.	This region has no snow because cold Antarctic air is warmed when it crosses the ocean.
mining		
manufacturing		
urban centers		

Reading-Writing Connection

On a separate sheet of paper, write a paragraph to compare and contrast the climate in your area with that of the humid subtropics described in the selection.

Skill: Problem–Solving Pattern

BACKGROUND INFORMATION

In "Wiping Out Yellow Fever," you will learn how the work of several scientists in different times and places finally solved the problem of a disease called yellow fever. There are many ways to solve problems in science. Most scientists begin by observing nature. They record and classify what they see. They use logic, and they plan experiments. They also come up with an overall explanation for what they see and learn.

SKILL FOCUS: Problem–Solving Pattern

Scientific advances usually come slowly. Often one scientist solves one part of the problem. Other scientists, working in different places, solve other parts of the problem. Each new scientist builds on the work of earlier ones.

When reading how scientific problems are gradually solved, ask yourself these questions.

- What was the basic problem?
- Who was the first scientist to work on the problem?
- What did the first scientist discover?
- Who was the next to work on the problem, and what did he or she learn?
- How did each new scientist use the work of the scientist who went before?

▶ Think of a serious medical problem that scientists today are trying to solve. Write the problem on the Sequence Chart. Then, in the next two boxes, describe two parts of the problem that scientists have already solved.

1. Scientists are trying to

2. They already learned

3. They already learned

CONTEXT CLUES: Details

The **details** in sentences surrounding an unknown word can often serve as context clues. These details can help you figure out the meaning of new words. In the sentences below, look for details that help you understand the meaning of the word *injected*.

> In 1796, he **injected** a young boy with cowpox germs. He forced the germs into the boy's body through a hollow needle.

If you don't know the meaning of *injected*, the details *forced the germs into the boy's body* and *hollow needle* help you figure it out.

▶ Circle the details that help show the meaning of *fatal* in the following sentences.

> In the past, yellow fever killed many people in Central America, South America, Africa, and on tropical islands. The discoveries of several scientists helped wipe out this **fatal** disease.

As you read the selection, look for details to help you understand the meanings of the underlined words *control*, *established*, and *sanitation*.

Strategy Tip

As you read "Wiping Out Yellow Fever," use the headings to identify the scientists whose work helped wipe out yellow fever. Think about how each scientist built on the work of an earlier one.

158   LESSON 52   Problem-Solving Pattern

Wiping Out Yellow Fever

YELLOW FEVER IS A DISEASE caused by a germ. Yellow fever can damage the liver and cause the sick person's skin to take on a yellow color. The disease usually begins with fever, dizziness, headache, and muscle aches. The sick person sometimes falls into a coma and dies.

In the past, yellow fever killed many people in Central America, South America, Africa, and on tropical islands. The discoveries of several scientists helped to wipe out this fatal disease.

Edward Jenner

Edward Jenner (1749–1823) was the first scientist to use **vaccination** (VAK sə NAY shən) to protect people from disease. In vaccination, a doctor injects people with a weakened form of a disease. These injected germs alert the body to make special cells to fight the disease. If the vaccinated person then gets the strong form of the disease, the body can fight it off. The vaccination gives them **immunity** (i MYOON ə tee) to the disease.

Jenner was an English doctor. He had watched many people die from a disease called smallpox. Jenner noticed that those people who had had cowpox never got smallpox. Cowpox was a disease similar to smallpox, but it was much milder. Jenner concluded that the cowpox germ protected people from getting smallpox.

In 1796, he injected a young boy with cowpox germs. He forced the germs into the boy's body through a hollow needle. A few months later, he injected the boy with smallpox germs. The boy never developed smallpox.

Jenner had found a way to stop the spread of smallpox. At first, people were afraid to try vaccination, but soon this new way to prevent smallpox was saving lives around the world.

Louis Pasteur

Other scientists were inspired by Jenner's work, and they began searching for new **vaccines** (vak SEENZ) to protect people from disease. Jenner had vaccinated people by using weaker germs from a less serious disease. In 1881, French scientist Louis Pasteur (1822–1895) took Jenner's work a step further. He found a way to take powerful germs and make them weaker. Then he began experiments using sheep and chickens.

Pasteur divided the animals into two groups. He injected one group with weakened germs. The other group of animals was not injected. They were the <u>control</u> group in the experiment. The animals that were not injected usually caught the serious disease and died. The animals that were injected did not catch the disease.

By 1885, Pasteur was ready to battle a deadly human disease—rabies (RAY beez). First he made a weakened form of the rabies germ. Using this vaccine, he saved the life of a 9-year-old boy who had been bitten by a dog with rabies.

Carlos Finlay

Now scientists were eager to find the germ that caused yellow fever. If they found it, perhaps they

SCIENCE

could use a vaccine to stop the spread of this deadly disease. Unfortunately no one knew what caused the disease. Many scientists believed that bedding and clothing from infected persons spread yellow fever.

In 1881, however, Carlos Finlay (1833–1915), a Cuban doctor, had a new idea. He believed that mosquitoes carried the yellow fever germ. Finlay tested his idea and wrote about his work in 1886. Unfortunately he did not prove his idea to other scientists. They ignored his work for years. Then an American doctor named Walter Reed finally proved that Finlay was right.

Walter Reed

In 1900, the U.S. Army chose a group of men to study yellow fever in Cuba. The disease had recently swept across the island, causing hundreds of deaths. Dr. Walter Reed (1851–1902) headed the group of three doctors who made the study.

At that time, the U.S. Army still believed that bedding and clothing spread the disease. Reed tested this idea. He watched and questioned hundreds of people who had the disease. Then he looked at their bedding and clothing under a microscope. He found no evidence that these items carried disease.

Luckily Reed was working in the home country of Carlos Finlay who still strongly believed that mosquitoes spread yellow fever. He finally persuaded Reed to test the idea. To work on this problem, Reed had mosquitoes bite people who had yellow fever. He then let these same mosquitoes bite some of his fellow doctors and several soldiers who had volunteered for the experiment. All of these coworkers caught yellow fever. One of them died. This daring experiment <u>established</u> proof that certain mosquitoes carry yellow fever.

William Gorgas

The next step was to find out how to get rid of the mosquitoes that carried yellow fever. William Gorgas (1854–1920), a U.S. Army doctor, knew where mosquitoes breed. Their breeding areas include trash heaps, garbage dumps, unused wells, old tin cans, puddles, ponds, and swamps. With this information, he began a program to clean up garbage and other wastes in Cuba that promoted the disease. This <u>sanitation</u> program helped stop the **epidemic** (ep ə DEM ik) of yellow fever. An epidemic is a widespread disease. Gorgas then went on to Panama to wipe out yellow fever there. His work in Panama saved the workers who were building the Panama Canal.

Max Theiler

The final step in solving the yellow fever problem took scientists back to the discoveries of Jenner and Pasteur. Could scientists now find the yellow fever germ in infected mosquitoes? Could they make a weaker form of the germ and use it for vaccinations?

Max Theiler (1899–1972), a South African doctor working in the United States, achieved this final step. In the 1930s, he created a weak form of the yellow fever germ. For more than 20 years, he continued to improve his vaccine. Because of his work, doctors could now protect people from yellow fever even if mosquitoes that carried the disease remained.

Today yellow fever is under control in most of the world. Although doctors cannot cure the disease, they can prevent its spread. Vaccinations and better sanitary conditions are their main weapons.

1. In what areas of the world did yellow fever occur?

   _____

   _____

2. What is vaccination?

   _____

   _____

   _____

3. What does it mean if you have immunity to a disease?

   _____

   _____

4. How much time passed between Jenner's vaccine for smallpox and Pasteur's vaccine for rabies?

   _____

   _____

   _____

5. Where did Walter Reed study yellow fever?

   _____

6. Why was it lucky that the U.S. Army had chosen Cuba as the place for Reed to do his study?

   _____

   _____

   _____

7. Fill in the correct word in each sentence below.

   sanitation   control   established

   a. Scientists use a _____ group so they can compare the effects of people getting a medicine and people not getting a medicine.

   b. Once scientists have _____ the cause of a disease, they can work on preventing or curing it.

   c. Good _____ means keeping an area clean so that diseases cannot spread.

CRITICAL THINKING

1. Explain why Louis Pasteur needed a group of animals that were not injected with weakened germs in his experiments.

   _____

   _____

   _____

2. Explain why vaccinations are an important method to fight the spread of diseases.

   _____

   _____

   _____

3. Discuss why it is important for scientists to publish and share results of their experiments.

   _____

   _____

   _____

4. Explain why people alive today should feel grateful to Edward Jenner.

   _____

   _____

   _____

Use the information in the selection to complete the chart below. In the Problem column, write one or more questions that each scientist tried to answer. In the Findings column, write the answer that the scientist found to each question. The first row is done for you.

How Scientists Solved the Problem of Yellow Fever		
Scientist	**Problem**	**Findings**
Edward Jenner	Can injecting a person with weak germs protect the person from a similar, stronger disease?	Injecting people with weak cowpox gems can protect them from deadly smallpox.
Louis Pasteur		
Carlos Finlay		
Walter Reed		
William Gorgas		
Max Theiler		

Reading-Writing Connection

Think about a problem that affected life in your school or your community. On a separate sheet of paper, write a paragraph explaining how the problem was solved. Describe the steps that were taken.

Skill: Reading a Graph

BACKGROUND INFORMATION

In "Bar Graphs and Line Graphs," you will read about different kinds of graphs. An old saying says that a picture is worth a thousand words. In a way, that explains why graphs are so popular. A graph gives a picture of information. That way, the information is clear and easy to understand. The picture information in graphs usually takes the form of lines, bars, or circles.

SKILL FOCUS: Reading Graphs

A **graph** shows information in a visual way. Many graphs show the differences between numbers or amounts at different times or places. Some graphs use bars to compare amounts. Other graphs use lines to show how number facts change over time.

The information on a graph is easy to see and understand. You can find information on a graph much more quickly than you can find the same information in a paragraph. You can also quickly compare amounts by comparing the bars or lines on a graph.

To use a graph, first read its **title**. The title tells what kinds of information are shown on the graph. Also pay attention to the **labels** along the bottom and up the side of the graph. The labels help you find the information you need.

▷ Look at the bar graph below. Read the title and the labels. Then answer the questions.

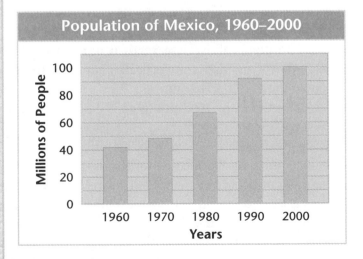

What is the title of the graph?

_____

What do the labels say?

_____

About how many people lived in Mexico in 1980?

_____

In what year did Mexico have almost 50 million people?

_____

WORD CLUES

When you read the following selection, pay special attention to the important words *horizontal bar graph*, *vertical bar graph*, *double bar graph*, *line graph*, *vertical axis*, and *horizontal axis*. Understanding these words will help you interpret information shown in graphs.

Strategy Tip

In "Bar Graphs and Line Graphs," you will read about three types of bar graphs and one type of line graph. Read the title of each graph before studying the graph itself. Learn what the labels on the graph mean.

Bar Graphs and Line Graphs

Graphs give a picture of information, or data. They help you to understand information by presenting it visually.

Horizontal Bar Graphs

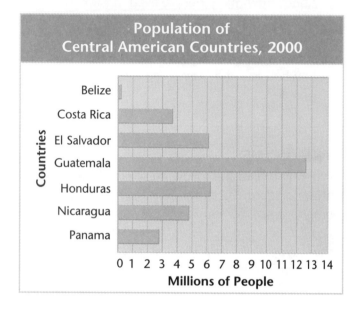

Population of Central American Countries, 2000

This is a **horizontal bar graph**. The bars that show data run across the graph from left to right.

The first thing that you should read is the title. The title tells what kind of information is shown in the graph. The title of this graph is *Population of Central American Countries, 2000*.

The two sides of the graph that give information are called the **vertical axis** and the **horizontal axis**. The vertical axis runs up and down. The horizontal axis runs from left to right.

It is important to read the labels for each axis before you read the rest of the graph. In this graph, the vertical axis is labeled *Countries*. It lists the countries whose populations are given. The horizontal axis is labeled *Millions of People*. It shows every number from 0 through 14. Each number stands for millions. The number 2 stands for 2 million people. The number 8 stands for 8 million people.

When you read a bar graph, look at each bar. In this graph, the length of each bar shows the population of one country. For example, one bar

shows that Honduras has a population of just over 6 million people. Another bar shows that Guatemala's population is over 12 million people.

This bar graph is more useful than a list of numbers because you can quickly compare the populations of the countries. It is easy to see that Belize has the smallest population. Guatemala has the largest population. You can also see that there are three countries whose populations are greater than 6 million people. Because the bars for Honduras and El Salvador are about the same length, you know that they have populations that are about the same.

Vertical Bar Graphs

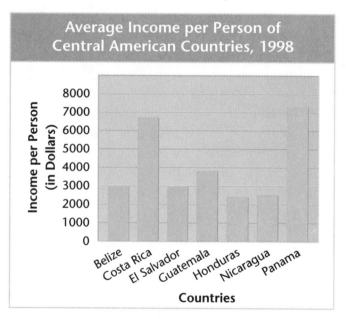

Average Income per Person of Central American Countries, 1998

The graph above is a **vertical bar graph**. The bars that show data are vertical. They run up and down the graph, like columns.

The title tells that this graph shows the 1998 average income per person in Central American countries. Average income is figured by dividing each country's total income for the year 1998 by the number of people living in the country. The vertical axis is labeled *Income per Person*. This is the amount of income in dollars. The horizontal axis is labeled *Countries*. Each bar shows the average income per person of a country. The graph shows that Panama has the greatest average income per person. Belize and El Salvador have average incomes per person that are about the same. Honduras and Nicaragua have the smallest average income per person.

Double Bar Graphs

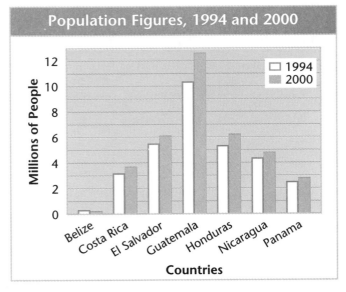

Population Figures, 1994 and 2000

The graph above is a **double bar graph**. It has two bars for each country shown. A double bar graph shows a comparison. This graph compares the populations of each country at two different periods of time.

Read the title of the graph. Then read the labels on the vertical axis and the horizontal axis. There is also a key on this graph. The key tells what the bars stand for. The white bars stand for the 1994 populations of the countries. The green bars stand for the 2000 populations of the countries.

A double bar graph can show a great deal of information. This one shows the population of seven countries in both 1994 and 2000. It also shows that the population of most countries has increased from 1994

to 2000 and which countries had the greatest increases. Guatemala had the greatest increase in its population.

Line Graphs

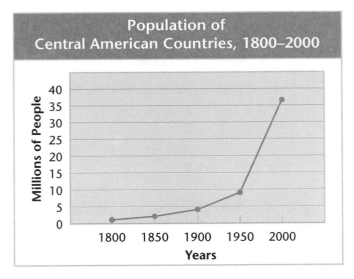

Population of Central American Countries, 1800–2000

The graph above is a **line graph**. Dots are used to show the population of all Central American countries at certain times. The dots are connected with straight lines. By connecting the dots, it is easy to tell the pattern of population change over a period of time. Line graphs are used to show change.

The title of this line graph is *Population of Central American Countries, 1800–2000*. Like the bar graphs, it has a vertical axis and a horizontal axis. Both are labeled. Using this graph, you can easily see that the population of Central America steadily increased between 1800 and 1950. You can also see that the increase between 1800 and 1850 was much smaller than the increase between 1900 and 1950. You can find that the population passed the 3 million mark sometime between 1850 and 1900. You can also see that the population grew almost four times between 1950 and 2000.

COMPREHENSION

1. What does the title of a graph tell?

_____

_____

2. Identify the three types of bar graphs discussed in this selection.

_____

_____

3. Explain what a double bar graph shows.

_____

_____

4. The titles of two graphs are listed below. Underline the title that is probably a line graph.

Population of European Countries

Daily High Temperature in Central America

CRITICAL THINKING

1. Explain why the numbers have to be equally spaced in a graph.

_____

_____

2. State some reasons that bar graphs are more useful than a list of numbers.

_____

_____

SKILL FOCUS: READING A GRAPH

A. Answer these questions. Use the graphs in the selection.

1. Which two countries have an average income per person that is greater than $ 5,000?

_____

2. About how many people lived in Honduras in 1994?

_____

3. What is the title of the double bar graph?

_____

B. Answer these questions. Use the graph below.

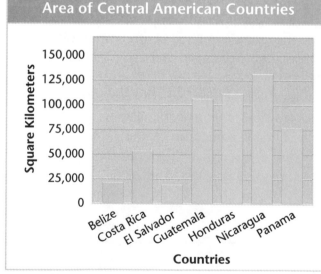

1. Which country has the greatest area?

_____

2. Which two pairs of countries have areas that are about equal?

_____

3. What is the area of Costa Rica?

_____

4. How many countries have areas of fewer than 100,000 square kilometers?

_____

Reading-Writing Connection

On a separate sheet of paper, write a paragraph to describe two situations at home or at school in which you could show information on a graph.

Skill: Accented Syllable and Schwa

When words contain two syllables, usually one of the syllables is stressed, or accented, more than the other when you pronounce it. For example, the first syllable in the word *picnic* is said with more stress than the second syllable. In most dictionaries, the **accent mark** (') is placed at the end of the syllable that is said with more stress. For example: *pic' nic*

Words that have three syllables usually are accented on one of the first two syllables. When you are trying to pronounce a word with three syllables, say the word with more stress on the first syllable. If the word does not sound right, say it again, giving the most stress to the second syllable. This will help you in deciding how to pronounce the word. For example: *beau' ti ful*

A. Say each of the following words to yourself. Write an accent mark after the syllable that should be stressed.

1.	thun der	8.	syl la ble	15.	sat in
2.	moc ca sin	9.	top ic	16.	con tin ue
3.	sol dier	10.	ter ri ble	17.	ru by
4.	prac tice	11.	am ber	18.	va por
5.	Co lum bus	12.	ex am ple	19.	con di tion
6.	in form	13.	trop i cal	20.	dis com fort
7.	dif fi cult	14.	ma chine	21.	re mem ber

The vowels *a, e, i, o,* and *u* can all have the same sound. This is a soft sound like a short *u* pronounced lightly.

1. Pronounce *around*. Did the *a* sound like a soft, short *u*? _____

2. Pronounce *harden*. Did the *e* sound like a soft, short *u*? _____

3. Pronounce *animal*. Did the *i* sound like a soft, short *u*? _____

4. Pronounce *collect*. Did the *o* sound like a soft, short *u*? _____

5. Pronounce *circus*. Did the *u* sound like a soft, short *u*? _____

This short, soft *u* sound is called the **schwa** sound. In dictionary respellings, the symbol ə stands for the schwa sound. If you look up the word *lament* in the dictionary, you will find it respelled as (lə ment').

B. Say each of the words below to yourself. Write an accent mark after the syllable that is accented. Then circle the letter that stands for the schwa sound.

1.	a cross	5.	cor al	9.	fall en
2.	com pel	6.	a light	10.	com mon
3.	but ton	7.	pan da	11.	li on
4.	car a van	8.	prob a bly	12.	car rot

LESSON 55

Skill: Main Idea—Stated or Unstated

When you read for information, you often find the main idea of each paragraph stated in a sentence. The supporting details, which give more information about the main idea, are found in the rest of the paragraph.

Sometimes the main idea of the paragraph is not stated. You may need to figure out, or infer, the main idea yourself. To do this, think about the supporting details. Then think of a sentence that summarizes them.

Read the following selection. Think about whether the main idea of each paragraph is stated or unstated.

Horses

1. There are more than 150 breeds and types of horses and ponies. The breeds vary greatly in size, strength, and speed. The smallest breed is the Falabella, which grows only 30 inches (75 centimeters) high. The largest breed is the Shire, which may measure more than 68 inches (170 centimeters) high.

2. Percherons, a kind of draft horse, once pulled heavy plows on farms. Other draft horses, such as Belgians, were used to haul freight wagons from town to town. Suffolk, a smaller draft horse, pulled milk wagons.

3. Southern plantation owners developed the American saddle horse and the Tennessee walking horse for pleasure riding. The owners wanted mounts that were comfortable to ride. Tennessee walking horses are especially noted for their comfortable running walk and smooth and easy pace. Morgans were originally used as harness horses for pulling carriages. After the automobile became popular, breeders developed the Morgan into an excellent pleasure riding horse.

4. Horses that roam freely in parts of the western United States are called wild horses. At one time, they were actually tame horses. Spanish explorers and cowhands of the Old West rode these horses. The horses escaped from their owners and eventually formed bands. In the early 1900s, more than 2 million of these horses roamed the West. Then people rounded up many of them to make room for farms and ranches. About 20,000 wild horses roam the West today.

A. For each paragraph, if the main idea is stated, write the word *stated* on the line. If the main idea is unstated, choose a sentence from the list below that gives the main idea of the paragraph. Write the letter of the correct main idea on the line.

   a. Draft horses are the tallest and heaviest group of horses.

   b. Draft horses once supplied much of the power needed for jobs that trucks and tractors do today.

   c. Federal laws now prohibit the killing of wild horses.

   d. The most popular breeds used for pleasure riding include the American saddle horse, the Tennessee walking horse, and the Morgan.

   e. Morgan horses were also used in harness racing.

   Paragraph 1. _____   Paragraph 2. _____   Paragraph 3. _____   Paragraph 4. _____

B. Now go back to the paragraphs that have a stated main idea. Circle the sentence in each paragraph that states the main idea.

168 LESSON 55 Main Idea—Stated or Unstated

Skill: Making Inferences

To answer the questions that follow the selection below, you will have to **infer**, or figure out, the answers. In order to infer, you need to put together what you read in the selection with what you already know.

Emma Lazarus

Emma Lazarus was born in 1849. As a child, she was different from her six sisters and brothers. She was not interested in sports and games. She was serious and frail. More than anything, she wanted to write great poetry. She read the work of famous poets and dreamed that someday her poetry would be like theirs.

When Emma was older, she went to Ward's Island. There she worked tirelessly to help the refugees who were streaming into New York City. Many of these people had been persecuted in their own countries. Now they came to the United States seeking freedom. Emma felt sorry for them and started a group to aid them.

Emma continued to write poetry. She became famous as more and more people read her work.

One day, she was asked to help raise money for the pedestal of the Statue of Liberty that was to be placed on Bedloe's Island in New York Harbor. Famous writers were asked to contribute pieces from their writings to be sold at auction. Emma agreed to help with the project. She decided to write a sonnet about the statue itself.

Emma Lazarus's poem, "The New Colossus," became famous around the world. In 1903, her words were engraved on the pedestal of the statue. Millions of immigrants coming to the United States in search of a new life read the stirring words. For the immigrants, the poem became as much of a symbol as the statue of a new land waiting for them, a land full of promise for a new beginning.

> Give me your tired, your poor,
> Your huddled masses yearning to breathe free,
> The wretched refuse of your teeming shore.
> Send these, the homeless, tempest-tossed to me,
> I lift my lamp beside the golden door!

1. Why was Emma Lazarus sometimes called the "Champion of Immigrants"?

   _____

   _____

   _____

2. Why was it so fitting that Emma Lazarus's poem was chosen to be engraved on the pedestal of the Statue of Liberty?

   _____

   _____

   _____

3. Why was New York Harbor chosen as the site for the statue?

   _____

   _____

   _____

4. When do you think Emma Lazarus wrote her poem? How can you tell?

   _____

   _____

   _____

Skill: Recognizing Propaganda

A statement of fact can be checked and proven to be true. For example, *The Cupcakes' newest album has sold 10,000 copies.* A statement of opinion tells what someone believes or feels. For example, *The Cupcakes' newest album is the best album ever made.*

If people believe that their opinions are important enough, they may try to persuade others to agree with them. When people try to persuade others to believe something, do something, or buy something, they are using **propaganda**. Most advertisements use propaganda to convince people to buy a certain product. Propaganda is also used by political candidates to convince people to vote for them.

The different types of propaganda have names. Here are examples of three types.

1. **Name Calling:** This type of propaganda gives a bad name to people or products so that other people will avoid them.

   Example: *If you don't mind wrinkled shirts, buy Millers Wash-'n'-Wear Shirts.*

2. **Glad Names:** This type of propaganda states good things about the listeners or readers so that they will agree with what they hear or read.

   Example: *A smart person like you knows that Oatsies are good for you.*

3. **Testimonial:** This type of propaganda uses the name of a well-known person so that people will do a certain thing because the person they admire says that it is a good thing to do.

   Example: *Use Bubble-Glo Shampoo. Famous movie star Lulu Cleo says it is terrific.*

Read the following statements. On the first line after each, write the type of propaganda used. On the second line, write the words from the statement that make it that type of propaganda.

1. Stan Waters, Rookie of the Year, eats a bowl of Strackles every morning. You, too, can be a superstar! Switch to Strackles.

   _____

   _____

2. I am convinced that you, as intelligent, thoughtful, patriotic people, will vote for me in the coming election.

   _____

   _____

3. You can buy that one if you like, but it's a real gas-burner. The body is about as strong as a tin can. Come over here, and I'll show you a really good car.

   _____

   _____

4. If you want Lou Power to be class president, that's your business. However, I think you should know that Lou is a born liar.

   _____

   _____

5. Our survey shows that you are highly regarded in your business. Join other successful people who subscribe to our weekly newsletter, "Facts of Finance."

   _____

   _____

6. What is the secret of Tina Tappler's award-winning voice? She gargles three times a day with Phizzmore. Try it!

   _____

   _____

Skill: Skimming for Information

When you are looking for specific information in a selection you have already read, you don't need to reread every word. You can save a lot of time by **skimming** for the facts that you need.

If you have to answer factual questions, find the **key words** in the question. The key words will tell you what information or facts to look for. Then use the **headings** in the selection to help organize your search. Because you have already read the selection, you know what information is covered in the paragraphs that follow each heading. When you find the section that has the information that you are looking for, stop and reread that material. Look for the key words in your question. Remember to reread only as much as necessary to get the information that you need.

Read the following selection.

America's Favorite City

On the northern Pacific coast of California is one of the world's most interesting cities, San Francisco. It lies directly south of the Golden Gate Strait at the entrance to San Francisco Bay. San Francisco has a charm that makes it different from any other city. It is this special charm that attracts millions of tourists to the city each year.

Location and Climate

San Francisco is on a hilly peninsula that stretches 30 miles (48 kilometers) southward along San Francisco Bay. The city covers an area of 46 square miles (119 square kilometers). San Francisco also includes several islands in the Pacific Ocean and in San Francisco Bay. Alcatraz, an island in the bay, was once the site of a federal prison. It is now a famous tourist attraction.

San Francisco has a moderate climate. It is relatively mild in winter and cool in summer. The temperature rarely rises to 70 degrees Fahrenheit (21 degrees Celsius) or drops to 30 degrees Fahrenheit (−1 degrees Celsius). The sun shines in San Francisco an average of 66 of every 100 daylight hours. Nevertheless, San Francisco has become well known for its fog.

History

The Costanoan Indians lived in what is now the San Francisco area long before Europeans arrived. In 1542, Juan Cabrillo sailed past San Francisco Bay without noticing it, and, in 1602, Sebastian Vizcaino did the same. Fog that often lies along the Pacific coast probably prevented early European navigators from finding the entrance to

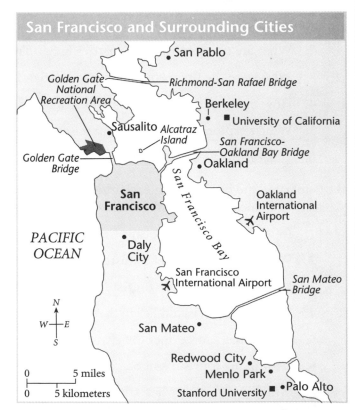

This map shows San Francisco and surrounding cities.

the bay. In 1579, the English explorer Sir Francis Drake also sailed by it.

In 1769, members of a Spanish expedition led by Gaspar de Portola traveled up the coast over land and became the first Europeans to climb the hills and see the bay. It was not until the late eighteenth century that Spaniards started a settlement there.

Government

San Francisco was incorporated as a city in 1850. The legislative branch of the government has an 11-member board of supervisors. The mayor and the chief administrative officer, who is appointed by the mayor, head the administrative branch. The voters elect the mayor and the members of the board of supervisors to four-year terms.

The city government gets most of its income from real estate taxes. The remaining funds that the city needs come from state and federal grants and from city bond sales.

Economy

Industry is a major source of income in San Francisco. Food processing is the chief industrial activity. Among the other important industries are shipbuilding and the manufacturing of clothing and other textile products. The city is one of the leading printing and publishing centers in the United States.

About a fifth of San Francisco's workers are employed in retail and wholesale trade. The biggest group are the workers who run the restaurants, hotels, and other businesses that serve the tourist trade. Almost 17 million tourists visit San Francisco yearly. They contribute close to $5 billion to the city's annual income.

A. **Read the following questions. Underline the key words that tell you the information you should look for. Then skim the headings in the selection. On the line provided, write the heading under which you would find the answer to each question.**

1. Who led the first European expedition to San Francisco Bay? _____

2. What are two important industries in San Francisco? _____

3. Who were the first people to live in the San Francisco area? _____

4. How many members are on the board of supervisors? _____

5. Which explorers missed San Francisco Bay? _____

6. What is the weather like in San Francisco? _____

B. **Underline the key words in each question. Then skim the paragraphs in the correct section to locate the facts that answer the question. Write the answer on the line.**

1. In what year did Europeans first see San Francisco Bay? _____

2. What is the city's chief industrial activity? _____

3. How much money do tourists spend in San Francisco each year? _____

4. Which famous island lies in San Francisco Bay? _____

5. From what source does the city government get most of its income? _____

6. How many tourists visit San Francisco yearly? _____

7. Which American Indian tribe lived in San Francisco? _____

8. What is the area of San Francisco?

Skill: Multiple-Meaning Words

When you look up the definition of an unfamiliar word in a dictionary, you may find that the word has several, or **multiple, meanings**. Read all of the definitions. Then find the meaning that fits the context of what you are reading. Always read all the definitions of a word before you decide on the correct meaning.

Read each dictionary entry word and its definitions below. Then read the three sentences, each with an underlined word, that follow. Find the correct meaning for the underlined word. Write the number of this meaning on the line. The first one is done for you.

bank   **1** a business place where money is held, exchanged, or loaned **2** the land along the sides of a river **3** a shallow place in a sea

   a. Ms. Lorca put her money in the <u>bank</u> for safekeeping. ___1___

   b. A ship ran aground on the sand <u>bank</u>. _____

   c. Kevin enjoyed sitting on the <u>bank</u> of the river and watching the ships go by. _____

cane   **1** the slender stem of some plants **2** a walking stick **3** thin strips of rattan used for the seats of chairs

   a. Mr. Pappas sprained his ankle. He had to use a <u>cane</u>. _____

   b. Mrs. Howe took her chairs to a shop to be mended. The <u>cane</u> seats had torn. _____

   c. Sara picked the ripe berries from the raspberry <u>cane</u>. _____

crop   **1** any farm product grown in the soil, such as cotton, corn, or fruit **2** a pouch in the neck of some birds where food is first digested **3** hair cut very short

   a. Mrs. Robinson, a farmer, had a fine <u>crop</u> of wheat this year. _____

   b. Insects and worms may be found in the <u>crop</u> of a robin. _____

   c. You will feel cooler in the summer if you have a close <u>crop</u>. _____

mine   **1** a pit from which precious stones, coal, or other minerals are taken by digging **2** a large supply or store of something **3** an explosive hidden in water or ground to destroy enemy ships or troops

   a. Mr. Putnam had a <u>mine</u> of rare, old paintings. _____

   b. Our battleships watched closely for <u>mines</u> during World War II. _____

   c. Three people were trapped in a coal <u>mine</u> without food for several days. _____

plain   **1** easy to understand **2** without beauty; homely **3** not fancy; not much decorated

   a. Mr. Morse was a very <u>plain</u> man. _____

   b. The teacher explained the problem until it was quite <u>plain</u> to the class. _____

   c. Bob served a <u>plain</u> cake for dessert. _____

yard   **1** a measure of length **2** a small space in front or back of a house or barn **3** a place in the open where work or business is carried on

   a. Marina planted some roses in the <u>yard</u> of her home. _____

   b. Mr. Sampson works in a railroad <u>yard</u>. _____

   c. It took five <u>yards</u> of cloth to make Rosa's new dress. _____

Skill: Using the Yellow Pages

> If you need the phone number of a certain business in your town, you can look up the business's number in the **Yellow Pages** of a phone book. Businesses are grouped together under headings. All of the same kinds of businesses are listed under the same heading and every heading is listed in alphabetical order. You can find the right heading by using the guide words at the top of each page. Businesses are listed alphabetically under the headings. After the business's name, its address and phone number are given. Some businesses place additional ads in the Yellow Pages.

A. Use the sample Yellow Page on page 175 to answer each question below.

1. Which travel agency is on North Country Road in Baldwin? _____

2. What phone number can you call to get a trailer to transport a pony? _____

3. Which travel agency has offices in two different towns? _____

4. What is the phone number for Janet Plummer's travel agency? _____

B. Circle the letter of the phrase that completes each sentence. Use the sample Yellow Page.

1. Using the Travel Bug advertisement, you can learn the following information:
   a. its address, its phone number, the kinds of trips it specializes in, and the length of the trips
   b. its address, its phone number, the kinds of trips it specializes in, and the year it was started
   c. its address, its phone number, the countries it specializes in, and the year it was started
   d. its address, its phone number, its prices, and the year it was started

2. You want a travel brochure about South America. You plan to be on Jericho Turnpike this afternoon. You can use the Yellow Pages to find out that
   a. the only travel agency on Jericho Turnpike is Go-Away Tours.
   b. you can call the Friendly Travel Service to ask if it has any information.
   c. two travel agencies are located on Jericho Turnpike.
   d. there are no travel agencies on Jericho Turnpike.

3. To get some information about ski trips, you can call
   a. Adventures in Travel at 555–2000 and Travel Bug at 555–1111.
   b. South American Adventures at 555–6265 and Travel Bug at 555–1111.
   c. Adventures in Travel at 555–2000 and Lake Grove Travel Center at 555–8199.
   d. Go-Away Tours at 555–0044 and Travel Associates at 555–8477.

Trailer Renting & Leasing (3) (cont'd)

Riverhead Campers
    3922 Jessup La Baldwin...........................555-0112
Trailer City
    903 Ketchum St Oakton...........................555-4438
U-Haul-It Trailer Rentals
    644 Hampton Bay Road Hampton............555-8428
    2000 Bellport Av Sayville.......................555-6347

Trailers—Horse
Long Island Horse Trailers
    404 Farmhouse Road Hampton.................555-3730

Travel Agencies & Bureaus
ADVENTURES IN TRAVEL
    See Our Ad
    243 Deer Park Av Baldwin.........................555-2000
Asian Travel Agency
    142 E. Broadway Sayville..........................555-6628
Budget Travel
    921 Norwalk Av Baldwin..........................555-8312
Foreign Travel Association
    1653 Jericho Trnpk Oakton.......................555-8316

Ginger Peachy Tours & Travel
    43 Scottsdale Av Sayville 555-3322
GO-AWAY TOURS, INC.
    See Our Ad
    1709 Jericho Trnpk Oakton....................555-0044
Inter Country Tours
    Individual or Group Travel Experts
    1888 Belllport Av Sayville......................555-1289
LAKE GROVE TRAVEL CENTER
    See Our Ad
    2400 Lake Grove Rd Hampton...............555-8199
Sayville Travel
    Central Shopping Plaza Sayville............. 555-0606
SOUTH AMERICAN ADVENTURES
    See Our Ad
    41 Brookhaven St Hampton....................555-6265
Sun and Fun Vacations
    819 N Country Rd Baldwin.................... 555-8133
Travel Associates
    945 Wheeler St Oakton..........................555-8477
TRAVEL BUG
    See Our Ad
    724 W Broadway Sayville 555-1111
Travel Bureau of South America
    6406 Wellwood Av Oakton 555-7000

CONTEXT CLUE WORDS

The following words are treated as context clue words in the lessons indicated. Each lesson provides instruction in a particular context clue type and includes an activity that requires you to use context clues to find word meanings. Context clue words appear in the literature, social studies, and science selections and are underlined or footnoted.

Word	Lesson
abundant	41
activated	13
altitude	21
arable	42
bigotry	12
boycott	30
brittle	2
casualty	12
catastrophe	43
condors	21
contracting	3
control	52
descent	21
destructive	43
distinguish	13
donated	20
drive	20
engrossed	1
established	52
expanding	3
feverishly	41
fibers	13
honorable	11
hull	2
irrigation	42
jagged	43
league	30
luster	32
makeshift	1
mammoths	50
nocturnal	22
online	20
paca	50
pierced	11
quarantined	22
refugee	1
repel	22
representatives	31
reserves	51
revenue	51
sanitation	52
scale	32
segregated	30
segregation	12
senators	31
serpent	50
spindly	41
sprint	11
staples	42
suction	3
territory	31
texture	32
tourism	51
watertight	2

CONCEPT WORDS

In lessons that feature social studies, science, or mathematics selections, words that are unique to the content and whose meanings are important in the selection are treated as concept words. These words appear in boldface type and are often followed by a phonetic respelling and a definition.

Word	Lesson
agriculture	31
alien	22
angle	44
anthropologist	21
Arabic numbers	14
axon	13
bridge	2
cinder-cone volcano	43
composite volcano	43
conduit	43
crater	43
decimal places	4
decimal point	4
dendrites	13
desegregate	12
double bar graph	53
economies	31
ecosystem	22
end point	44
epidemic	52
eruption	43
flagellum	3
habitat	22
haciendas	42
horizontal axis	53
horizontal bar graph	53
humid	51
immigrants	2
immunity	52
integrate	12
investigations	2
lava	43
line	44
line graph	53
line segment	44
long-term memory	13
magma	43
manufacturing	31
neurons	13
physical properties	32
pilgrimage	21
plantations	31
plateau	42
point	44
precious	32
prejudiced	12
ray	44
regenerate	3
Roman Numerals	14
semiprecious	32
shield volcano	43
short-term memory	13
subtropics	51
symbol	14
telegraph	2
tentacles	3
tropics	51
vaccination	52
vaccines	52
vent	43
vertex	44
vertical axis	53
vertical bar graph	53
working memory	13